The Business of Journalism

TEN LEADING REPORTERS AND EDITORS ON THE PERILS AND PITFALLS OF THE PRESS

Edited by William Serrin

The New Press
New York

Published by The New Press, New York, 2000
Distributed in the United States by
W.W. Norton & Company, Inc., New York

LIBRARY OF CONGRESS CATALOGING-IN-PUBLICATION DATA

The business of journalism : ten leading reporters and editors
on the perils and pitfalls of the press / edited by William Serrin.
p. cm.
ISBN 1-56584-581-1 (pbk.)
1. Press—United States. 2. Journalism—United States.
I. Serrin, William.
PN4738.B87 2000
071'.3—dc21 99-087926

The New Press was established in 1990 as a not-for-profit
alternative to the large, commercial publishing houses
currently dominating the book industry. The New Press
operates in the public interest rather than for private gain,
and is committed to publishing, in innovative ways, works
of educational, cultural, and community value that are
often deemed insufficiently profitable.

The New Press, 450 West 41st Street, 6th floor,
New York, NY 10036
www.thenewpress.com

PRINTED IN CANADA

9 8 7 6 5 4 3 2 1

Contents

To Judith Serrin,
without whose assistance
this book—yet another book—
would not have been finished.

Introduction

By William Serrin

A nasty, unreported truth about journalism is this: Journalism is a business. Journalists like to pretend this is not so, but it is. That journalism is a business is not by definition wrong. This is a business world, and bills, including those weekly or monthly checks to reporters, must be paid. I have worked at newspapers with money and newspapers without money, and the former is the place to be. Still, because it is a business, journalism is far less than the independent, courageous force that generations of journalists—reporters, editors, publishers, journalism educators—and journalism folklore claim it to be.

What this means for journalism and for democracy is a complex matter. One reason it is complex is that there are no written rules for what a newspaper, a magazine, or a radio or television news department will cover, or what these news institutions will not cover, or in what manner the coverage will be done. Rather, those decisions reflect a series of understandings, customs, traditions, and rules of journalism culture—most of it uncodified, except in journalism textbooks, to which no one pays much attention, in college or later—that have built up in the more than a century and a half since the beginnings of modern American journalism.

Everyone is in on this: the reporter, the editor, the producer, the anchorperson, the advertising salesperson, the journalism educator, the publisher, and, increasingly today, the market analyst. The rules go something like this:

Watch out when doing stories on people with money or position, or about businesses, meaning large businesses (small businesses don't matter much); be careful, especially about going too far with a story. Similarly, don't push too hard for stories on the poor, the homeless, the labor movement, or the working class. These, in most cases, go against a journalism corporation's demographics, because journalism increasingly wants to attract only upscale readers or viewers. Be careful when covering matters you know are of interest to the publisher, the station manager, or the network CEO, including their friends in the social world, charitable world, or corporate world. Don't be particularly venturesome. Stories outside the usual will be considered strange, even dangerous; most editors would rather run with the pack than strike out on their own. Finally, and this is especially true at smaller or medium-sized news organizations, be careful about proposing stories that are likely to take time. In journalism, as in other businesses, time is money. The more stories an editor can get out of a reporter, the happier the editor is; similarly, the more stories an editor can get out of a newsroom, the happier a publisher or station owner or network CEO will be.

The reporter, fearless and independent according to the folklore of journalism (composed of newsroom stories cherishingly passed by one generation of newspersons to the next, by journalism movies, and to some extent by journalism education and journalism history texts), likes to believe he or she is above the ruck. Not so. The business of journalism affects reporters as much as anyone. Most reporters want to get ahead, to make larger salaries, to become stars. To do this they must please their editors. To please their editors, reporters must obey the established, largely unwritten rules of the newsroom.

Another truth is that reporters and editors are, or soon become, like everyone else. They get tired, beaten down. They go soft, and go soft quickly. An editor who understood this was Joseph Medill Patterson, founder of the *New York Daily News* and member of the Medill-McCormick-Patterson journalism empire that at one time included the *Chicago Tribune,* the *Daily News,* the *Washington Times–Herald,* and *Newsday.* Journalists start out by challenging power, said Captain Patterson, who also once proclaimed that if he were a reporter, he would join a union. They are on the side of the people, and the people support them by buying their papers. But, the captain said, success makes the journalists wealthy, so they buy a station wagon (today, a sports utility vehicle), join the country club, and start spending time with people of power. These new friends don't seem so bad anymore. Gradually, the journalists stop taking the side of the people, and the readers wonder what happened. The captain knew this was true, because this is essentially what happened to him.

Because they are often so feckless, reporters are often the greatest censors. I have seen this many times. "I'll never get this into the paper," a reporter will say. Or, "They'll never let me print that." Who are "they," you might ask. "They" are the editors and owners for whom the reporter works. And the truth is, sometimes "they" probably won't let the reporter get a particular story into the paper or on the air. But that is only the first problem in this matter. The second is, the reporter gives up trying, the beginning of journalism self-censorship.

The editor is the same, but more so. The editor is often a former reporter who got out of reporting by becoming an editor. Usually the editor became tired of being a reporter—running around in the gloom of night, working the telephones, taking the picture of the deceased child off the fireplace mantel—and escaped by crossing the divide that separates reporters from editors, a far greater newsroom divide than separates editorial operations from business and advertising.

The task of the editor, generally, is to protect, not attack; to soften, not harden. In essence, editors are gatekeepers, whose responsibility it is to insure that stories that come through them do not go outside the conventions of journalism, do not rough up anyone of power or position, do not show passion, and do not betray the reporter's code of objectivity.

To both reporter and editor, the adage of Peter Finley Dunne—Mr. Dooley—that the job of the journalist is to comfort the afflicted and afflict the comforted, is newsroom claptrap. (This is also true in most of journalism education. I once quoted Mr. Dooley to members of the faculty with which I am associated, and was essentially laughed out of the place.)

You see these things all the time in the newsroom.

At one newspaper, I sat next to a reporter who read much of what he wrote—not just a key paragraph, say, or a technical matter—back to his sources; official sources, not ordinary people.

"Why are you doing this?" I finally asked, having witnessed this many times.

"I can't afford to make a mistake," the reporter, an otherwise fine man, said. And he never, or hardly ever, made a mistake. But he didn't print much that was any good, either.

I once worked at a newspaper at which an important editor would sometimes wander back to the book-review section, put a book on the reviewer's table, and say, gently, "Be kind." And the reviewer, while he privately detested the important editor, would.

I once read of a reporter for a national newsmagazine who had quit after many years there. Someone asked him why, and he said he had spent his career cozying up to important people to get them to tell him things, but that one day, in a dazzling moment of epiphany, he had realized that all the important, moneyed people he had spent so much time cozying up to weren't telling him a thing. He went off to run a bed-and-breakfast on the coast of California.

Reporters like to blame others, particularly editors, but they can't blame everything on the editors. A reporter can't quit every day, or even every day threaten to quit. But sometimes, as Sydney H. Schanberg tells us, reporters are faced with putting their jobs on the line, and most times they don't.

The editor and news director are in on the game, too, often in a more important way than the reporter is. They want to get along—with other editors, including their bosses, and, when they see them, with the owners.

The editor also knows what the unstated understandings are. Every editor knows that the killing of a white, college-educated career woman is more important in the news that the killing of a black, teenaged welfare mother. Sometimes orders, clearly or obliquely stated, come down from owners who want to support a downtown development that, "coincidentally," will increase the value of the owners' property. Sometimes top advertisers will pass the word that they do not want their names mentioned in any unfavorable light. In 1911, Will Irwin wrote, in his groundbreaking series "The American Newspaper" in *Collier's,* that "the custom of suppressing news, of slanting news policies, at the request or command of the advertiser, originated not so much with the advertiser himself as with the solicitor of the newspaper." Sometimes editors or news directors go after every angle on a crime story far beyond the story's inherent news value, because each additional twist adds to sales or ratings. Sometimes newsroom managers will close a foreign bureau or call off a reporting trip across the country because the travel budget is used up. So stories go uncovered. Sometimes a reporter quits, and the slot is left vacant, perhaps for months or more, to save money. More stories go uncovered.

The impact of the business side of journalism is only magnified as media companies become larger, and as chains buy out independent newspapers and stations across the country, and huge media companies merge, as demonstrated in January 2000 with the multibillion dollar merger of America Online with Time Warner. The practices that other large national corporations use have spread to journalism. Corporations are hierarchical, and journalists not only have accepted, but honor, hierarchy. National policy overrides local conditions; the corporate headquarters of one chain, for example, required all of its newspapers to run a page on auto racing, even though auto racing was not a popular sport in many of the cities within the papers' circulation. The journalism conglomerates train their managers the way other corporations do, rotating them through different offices every several years, sending them to the next stop before they learn enough about the community to be effective journalists there. The historic separation of advertising and news is breaking down; the advertising and production wings of cereal companies work together, so why not the advertising and news departments of newspapers? Much was made in late 1999, as it should have been, of the *Los Angeles Times's* grievous error in agreeing to split profits of a magazine issue on the new Staples Center with the center's management. But many news organizations are on the path in organizing special sections and other arrangements for advertisers.

The head office also can, and generally does, establish (on the advice of market analysts) what the profits, and profit margins, of each outlet must be. This is the case even though the home office and the market analysts often do not have the vaguest idea of what might be sufficient profits for the chain's outlets to do good journalism and to assist the communities in which they are located.

Finally, the values of business are more and more becoming the values of the American newsroom. All the great editors have been and are seat-of-the-pants people. They knew the value of making money, but they did not let money run them. Now, the values once associated with Wall Street, with the kind of people journalists covered, are becoming the values of the people doing the covering. Bigger salaries; bigger and faster cars; fine food and fancy clothes; vacations to Europe, Asia, and tropical islands; the larger office; the house in an upscale suburb—all these are now in substantial degree the values of reporters and editors turning out the nation's newspapers, magazines, and radio and television programs.

In journalism, as in many other fields—politics, government, the military, business, education, unions; in fact, most of life—journalists have to decide at some point what kind of professionals they are going to be. Are they going to do the work they think is most needed, or the work that will get them the most attention from their bosses? Are they going to go for substance, or for flash and celebrity? Will they keep quiet when they see a shoddy piece of work pass, or will they fight for higher standards, even if the challenge provokes their bosses? Do they want to be known for their work, or for being known?

This book, which began as a speakers' series at New York University in the spring of 1999, sponsored by The New Press and the NYU journalism department, is designed to examine in depth the business of journalism and what this means. To investigate these matters, The New Press and the journalism department, with the support of the NYU law school, invited nine prominent American journalists of varying interests and experience to examine the business of journalism and particularly the censorship, including self-censorship, that exists because journalism is a business, and what might be done to attack this situation.

It took courage for the authors to write these pieces, for in most cases they too work for large media institutions. A number of other well-known reporters and media critics declined to participate in this series. Each said it was a good idea, but each said no.

Do the ubiquitous "they" truly have the power most journalists accord them? The authors of the eight lectures in this book outline some of the pressures they have encountered during careers that total several hundred years of work at some of the country's most noted and respected news organizations. Among them, the writers have won two Pulitzer Prizes and published more than a dozen books.

Pat and Tom Gish are among the last of the breed of independent weekly newspaper publishers. Their lives have been examples of what happens when you don't operate your paper solely as a business. In their piece, they talk about the difficulties in attempting to tell the truth in a community that did not want to hear it, and about what can happen to journalists who do not practice self-censorship. Advertisers pulled out, the Gishes were snubbed, and the paper's office was torched by an enemy angry over a story. They never missed an issue.

Ronnie Dugger, a former editor of the maverick magazine the *Texas Observer,* sees the dangers of the increasing control of journalism by large entertainment-media corporations. News divisions are such a small part of these operations, Dugger says, that they often have little power. And reporters who think they have freedom of the press can have their work silenced by superiors afraid to confront their bosses or powerful forces in their communities.

E. R. Shipp, ombudsman of the *Washington Post* and a member of the journalism faculty at Columbia University, tells about the politics of the *New York Times* newsroom and the strategies she learned to get into the paper stories about issues she felt were important, even if her editors did not agree. A good journalist must learn how to maneuver around the rules of the newsroom, she says. But she concedes that she avoided doing some good stories because she thought she would be stereotyped "a black reporter." And she says that often, reporters just stop fighting.

It was James Warren of the *Chicago Tribune,* who, new to Washington but with an old-fashioned police reporter's eye, exposed the nefarious practice of journalists accepting speaker fees, often of many thousands of dollars, from organizations they cover or might be assigned to cover. The journalists have not reacted well to being reported upon. Warren continues his exposés. He also describes how difficult it is to bring change to Washington journalism, which, from the beginning of the country's history, has focused on leaders and institutions.

Vanessa Williams is an urban-affairs reporter at the *Washington Post* and immediate past president of the National Association of Black Journalists. She worries that newsrooms remain white ghettos, increasingly out of touch with a country that is becoming stunningly diverse. The disparity, she says, leads to a censorship, sometimes intentional, sometimes unintentional, of points of view not familiar to white reporters and editors. And she finds it curious that the white youths who shot up Columbine High School in Colorado were described in the press as members of a clique, while minority youths who might be involved in similar actions would probably be described as members of a gang.

Sydney H. Schanberg—once an editor of mine, and a fine editor he was—deplores how journalism, conducting itself as a business, is lowering its standards and is now willing to investigate people's private lives and exploit that information for circulation and financial gain. The public won't learn the details about that, he says, because the nation's news outlets refuse, being the businesses that they are, for the most part, to cover themselves. For three years, Schanberg, one of the nation's most distinguished reporters and writers, approached top news organizations about securing a position as a media writer who would give journalism the same scrutiny that journalism is supposed to give other areas of American life. He found himself respected, but not wanted.

The businessman in this group is Jay Harris, publisher of the muckraking magazine *Mother Jones.* Harris notes that, to some extent, journalism has to be a business; he knows this because it is his job to help *Mother Jones* make money to pay its bills. Because the magazine is set up as a nonprofit foundation, however, editors can edit to deliver the news, not deliver the profit. That's not the way most of the industry works. Harris also talks, most originally, about what he calls journalism's "master narrative," which shapes all news.

John Leonard, the talented critic and essayist, tells stories from his days as a reporter at the *New York Times,* as editor of its influential book review, and now as media critic at the CBS show *Sunday Morning.* He talks about the compromises that journalists often have to make; they have become, he says, "caged birds in a corporate canary cage." Leonard believes that no one can win every battle, but that the fight must be made.

The writers here are not, however, without hope. They are proud of their profession. They see the changes that are roiling journalism as an opportunity to do things in new, better ways. They do not believe in focus groups and market research. They are firm believers that good writing and good storytelling trumps all, winning readers and viewers for even complicated issues. They know how important the profession is and will remain, and they know the power of the individual example. As E. B. White wrote, "As long as there is one upright man, as long as there is one compassionate woman, the contagion may spread and the scene is not desolate."

This book was the idea of André Schriffin, publisher of The New Press, and I thank him for that idea, and for both the privilege of organizing this lecture series and the responsibility of editing this book. I hope Schriffin's editors will allow me to say that he has shown time and again in his long and distinguished career that the phrase "an honorable publisher" need not be an oxymoron.

Josephus Daniels, long the publisher of the Raleigh, North Carolina, *News and Observer,* once said, only partially in jest, that journalism is not an honorable profession. But it is. The thing is, it could be more honorable. I hope this book goes some way toward accomplishing that.

1.

We Still Scream

The Perils and Pleasures of Running a Small-Town Newspaper

By Pat and Tom Gish

"Freedom of the press," said the press critic A. J. Liebling, "belongs to those who own one." But as Pat and Tom Gish, owners and editors of the Mountain Eagle, *a six-thousand-circulation weekly in the eastern Kentucky town of Whitesburg, can testify, owning a newspaper comes with its own price. This is especially true when the owners of the paper have a view of journalism that challenges local truths.*

The Gishes purchased the Mountain Eagle *in 1957 and made it into a rare voice with the courage to speak out on behalf of miners and local residents against the coal companies, local businessmen, and other powers-that-be. "For forty-two years," said a former* Eagle *staff member, Thomas N. Bethell, "they have been the skunk at the party. They have been the little boy who not only notices but reports that the emperor has no clothes." Advertisers boycotted them, local residents shunned them, they received threats, and at one point the paper's offices were torched. In response, the Gishes changed the paper's long-standing motto, "It screams," to "It* still *screams."*

Tom Gish, the son of a Kentucky coal miner, had been a United Press reporter in the state capital of Frankfort before he bought the paper. Pat Gish had reported for the after-

noon daily in Lexington, Kentucky. Together they have made their paper into an important resource for people concerned about the fight against poverty in Appalachia, the fate of coal miners as the economy becomes more dependent on machines, the weaknesses of occupational safety and health laws, and the ravaging of the Cumberland Mountains by strip-mining. They champion those who otherwise would have no one on their side. And they do it in probably the most difficult of settings: in a part of the nation where, Bethell emphasized, exercising the right of free speech and free press has historically been hazardous.

The small-town newspaper editor willing to risk everything to publish that one important story is becoming a thing of the past. One major reason for this is the trend of consolidation that has hit small-town newspapers in recent years. Almost all weekly and small-town daily newspapers in Kentucky, for example, have been purchased by large corporations, most of them based outside the state. The same is true elsewhere.

Some twenty Kentucky newspapers were swallowed in one gulp recently by a publishing company financed by loans from the Alabama Teachers Retirement System. One of the newspapers in this buyout was another mountain newspaper that we have read and respected for many years. It offered good reporting, good editorials, and especially outstanding coverage of the county school system—by all measures one of the worst public school systems in America. For the past decade this newspaper has had perhaps the best coverage of any Kentucky school system, thanks to a gutsy reporter. Her stories detailed just about every kind of fraud and corruption and misuse of school funds you could find anywhere. One consequence of that school system's failure is that the children who attend its schools are among the most poorly educated in the country. Far too many students drop out or are pushed out of school and doomed to follow the path that leads about half the adults in eastern Kentucky to be functionally illiterate.

It was not a happy situation that the reporter wrote about. School officials much preferred the kind of puffery that assures parents that their kids are receiving educations equal to those elsewhere. Every kid is smarter than any other, and every school better than all others.

Not long after the chain took over the paper, we received a phone call from the reporter, who told us that as soon as she hung up she was getting in her car and leaving the community. What had happened? She was called in by the newspaper's new manager and told that she had to stop writing all those bad stories about the schools. She heard that her stories made people unhappy and that wasn't what the newspaper's owners wanted to do. "Happy news" makes people happy, and happy people make a prosperous community, they said.

She packed up and left town, and in the six months or so that have gone by since then, readers in that county have had little reason to be unhappy because of anything found in their newspaper. The sad truth is that happy news has become the prevailing philosophy in all too many community newspapers.

It is now possible for a small daily paper—and about 40 percent of the country's daily papers have a circulation under ten thousand—to be essentially a one-person news operation. That person receives the daily Associated Press report, downloads it into page layouts on a computer, and lays in the copy around the ads, often using headlines suggested by the AP. Thanks to the ever-improving wonders of computers, it is possible, even simple, for one person to use the AP and lay out a ten- or sixteen-page paper or more, and still have time left to write an obituary or two, check with the police on local crime or injury news, and type up some local news releases. That same person can then e-mail the pages to a press in another town, take a nap until the time nears for the printing run to be completed, drive over to pick up the papers, bring them back to town, and put them out on newsstands. The printer probably will take the copies to be mailed to the post office for him.

These newspaper developments are not all that different from what has happened to local radio. In many communities local stations with local news coverage are history. Satellite feeds of recorded music and national headlines now fill up most of the air time. Except for an occasional station break with local ads and maybe a local weather report, you would never know you were listening to a so-called "local" station. When money is spent, the dollars go into salaries for ad salesmen and business managers, not into local news coverage.

Censorship? Maybe—but not as a deliberate act. To engage in censorship you first have to know that an event or some circumstance has or is about to occur. If you don't cover news in the first place, is your lack of coverage censorship or just good business practice? We fear the answer is self-evident. The happier the news, the greater the amount of advertising. Newspapers, radio, or television—it's all the same. Outside ownership, reduced news coverage, happy news, lots more ads.

We have been at this business of community journalism for forty-two years. They have been years of great challenge, but also years of great satisfaction—the feeling, the knowledge, that we were doing something worthwhile, that we were happier where we were than we could possibly be in any other career choice.

We bought our newspaper, the *Mountain Eagle,* in 1957 when it was fifty years old. The paper is located in Whitesburg, the county seat of Letcher County, where coal mining was and still is the dominant industry. We brought to the community a combined twenty years of newspapering experience and a certain amount of smugness that we knew what news was. Pat had worked for ten years at the afternoon daily in Lexington, Kentucky, where her assignments included health, schools, city government, and the state legislature. For those same years Tom had worked as bureau manager of United Press at Frankfort, the state capital, reporting on state government and occasionally helping with coverage of the Derby and other Kentucky events.

There is no good answer as to why we bought the *Mountain Eagle,* other than that it was the paper Tom had read as a child growing up in a Letcher County coal camp, it was for sale, and we shared the dream of so many reporters of owning our own newspaper.

We are still surprised at our lack of knowledge about eastern Kentucky at that time. We didn't know that the coal economy was falling apart. We didn't know that one of every two mountain adults couldn't read or write. We didn't know that tens of thousands of mountain families had been plunged into the extremes of poverty, with children and adults alike suffering from hunger and some dying of starvation. We didn't know that mountain pride and independence caused mountain people to suffer in silence—they believed it was God's will that they live such destitute and, by national standards, hopeless lives. Like other practicing reporters in Frankfort, Louisville, and Lexington, we considered ourselves well-informed about Kentucky and its many parts. It was a real shock to find that we knew almost nothing about the mountain region of Kentucky and neither did our fellow newsmen elsewhere.

The *Mountain Eagle* in 1957 was like many other community newspapers in that it was owned by publishers who first and foremost were printers, not reporters. They made their living printing letterheads and business forms. The newspaper was put together after all the orders for printing had been taken care of. Little or no reporting was done. Instead there were long columns of weekly meeting reports from the Rotary Club, the Lions Club, the garden club, 4-H, and other clubs, and endless obituaries, often half a newspaper page long, in which every sermon was reprinted. News consisted mostly of columns of items from local community correspondents, mailed in from volunteer writers at Jenkins, Mayking, Kuz, Ice, Hot Spot, Kingdom Come, and a dozen other communities around the county.

With what we now recognize as either stupidity or ignorance, we set about doing what we knew how to do. We started reporting on public affairs in the county. As reporters we attended meetings of two school boards, three city councils, and the county governing body, known as the fiscal court. We wrote and printed detailed stories of what happened at those meetings. There were quotes of what public officials said, accounts of how members voted, and explanations of what was being considered—the kind of reporting commonplace in newspapers everywhere.

What we also did not know was that Letcher County officeholders were not accustomed to detailed public disclosure of their activities. School board meetings were considered gatherings of friends and allies. What the board did was regarded as private business. No reporters wanted, no news stories allowed. Several government agencies passed motions declaring their meetings off-limits to reporters. We found ourselves in a fight for fundamental freedom of the press, the right of the *Mountain Eagle* to attend and report on public government functions. It was a battle that took up much of our time and energies for a decade and it got downright nasty at times.

For the first few years we owned the *Eagle,* job printing was still a major portion of the newspaper's income. Fiscal court not only banned us from meetings but hit us financially by canceling all its printing contracts. Finally we turned the job printing back over to the paper's former owners and became newspaper publishers only. The county school board chairman tried to ban us from the board's meetings and told teachers, parents, and the public in general to boycott the *Eagle.* Don't buy it. Don't read it. Don't let it in your homes. The board of a city school system passed a resolution banning the *Eagle* from its meetings.

It would be nice to say that the community welcomed our reporting, but it didn't. Just about everything we wrote was treated with suspicion, often with disbelief. "Who paid you to put that in the paper?" was a taunt we often heard. Eventually we realized that the suspicions were not without reason. We learned that for years the paper had sold front-page stories to candidates for local offices. And we were confronted in one tense moment at the office by the county's leading criminal figure, a man with several shootings and convictions on his record. He wanted to buy that week's front page to advance his political candidate. "Name your price," he said as he displayed a giant wad of bills. We knew the man's reputation; we had heard stories about his foes who had disappeared. We were scared, and saying "no" to that man at that time, when the paper was having serious financial problems, was one of the toughest decisions we ever made. But, we said "no" and he left us alone. In fact, as our problems continued over the next several years, there were times when we would walk the two blocks from our office to the post office and we would be in such universal disfavor that no one on the street would speak to us except that man. He seemed to know what we were going through, and we shared the common bond of community shunning.

Whitesburg is a town of about seventeen hundred persons. It serves as the Main Street for the county's population of twenty-six thousand. The eastern border of Letcher County is also part of the Kentucky-Virginia border. Three of Kentucky's major rivers have their sources in Letcher County, so when you are there you are literally as far up the creek as you can get. For the past eighty-five years the local economy has been dominated by the ups and downs of coal mining. For the past forty years there has been a steady decline in coal mining employment as bigger and bigger machines have taken over the work of men. Coal employment has gone from eight thousand in the 1950s to a thousand miners today.

Whitesburg is the shopping center, the medical center, the banking center, and the legal center for the county, and it likes to think of itself as somehow not a part of the broader county population with all of the problems that go with 50 percent unemployment. The community folklore had been that coal mining would boom tomorrow, that there was no poverty, that our schools were the best, our homes the finest, our kids the brightest, our churches the best, God was in His heaven, and all was well. No inquiring reporters needed.

Shortly before we arrived in town, a special investigation by the U.S. surgeon general showed that adequate health care did not exist for most families in coal mining regions. As a result of that survey, the United Mine Workers of America union built a chain of splendid hospitals in the eastern coalfields, including one in Whitesburg. These hospitals recruited top graduates from the country's top medical schools. They engaged in a clinic practice at the hospitals, with the UMW paying doctor and hospital bills for miners and their families. Instantly coal miners had some of the best medical care in the United States. The Kentucky Medical Association called the UMW system "socialized medicine" and pressured the state legislature to pass laws allowing the miners to pick their own doctors and not be limited to those connected with the new hospitals. The *Eagle* spoke out in behalf of the miners and the new hospitals, and Tom went to Frankfort to talk with legislators and state officials whom he had known during his years as a reporter there. The legislature shelved the issue by referring the matter to a two-year study commission. Our local Buick-Pontiac-GMC-Goodyear dealer, a staunch conservative and the brother of a well-to-do nonunion coal operator, was opposed to the UMW's "socialized medicine." He canceled all his ads in the *Eagle*. With all those products, he was our largest advertiser, and the loss of that business just about destroyed the paper. That was just the beginning.

The problems of coal mine explosions and mine safety issues, coupled with the enormous environmental damage caused by strip-mining, became the targets of years of editorials and news reports in the *Eagle*. Bethlehem Steel Corporation, owner of the largest coal mines in our county, reacted by telling the Letcher County business establishment that the *Eagle* was a communist publication and should be put out of business.

In the early 1960s, when national attention focused on Appalachian poverty, there was talk of a new effort to help the region. The *Eagle* editorially urged development patterned after the Tennessee Valley Authority. Along with others, we proposed that coal be used to produce electricity that would be shipped by transmission lines to places such as New York City. This method also would save the cities money and ease their air pollution problems. This drew the anger of the American Electric Power Company, the public utility for most of eastern Kentucky and one of the largest in the nation. AEP sent representatives into Letcher County to visit every business establishment, urging them to withdraw advertising from the *Eagle* and cancel subscriptions because the publishers were communists. The power company did what it had urged others to do and canceled its own weekly ads.

We should have known—and exercised appropriate self-censorship—that America's giant utilities are not about to let anyone talk about public ownership of electrical generating plants. Communism, for sure.

It is hard to pinpoint who canceled what ad for what reason or at whose urging, but the paper declined to the point that it was often only four tabloid-size pages in the 1960s and early 1970s. We had one loyal advertiser during that period who saw issues much as we did. He was Ray Collins, an Old Regular Baptist minister who made his living as a bottler of Royal Crown Cola products. Collins supported the *Eagle* by purchasing a full-page ad every week for ten years. This paid us enough hard cash to buy newsprint and stay in business. I am happy to report that he did not waste his advertising dollars. His bottling firm climbed to the proud position of number one in per capita sales in the United States, and Collins delighted in spreading the word to local merchants about the effectiveness of *Eagle* advertising.

We are convinced that knowledge is power and that the more the *Eagle* can help inform its readers about both local and faraway developments that affect them, the more good things can happen. We decided very early that the coal industry had enough publicity people to put its views before the public, and we made it our business to be spokesmen for the coal miners who had to work in unsafe conditions and the landowners whose property was being destroyed by strip-mining or whose wells were being ruined by deep mining. We were also concerned about children who were not getting an adequate education, people who couldn't afford good health care, communities that didn't have adequate public water and sewer systems. These decisions, of course, were censorship of a sort. We used our limited space for the things we considered important.

Sometimes editors have to pick their fights, and that's what we did in the early 1960s concerning conditions in eastern Kentucky and other parts of Appalachia. We decided we would do what we could to show outside reporters and government officials how things really were and not how the local small-town establishment wanted people to think they were. When outsiders came to take a look, we put down what we were doing and escorted them to places we thought they ought to see. There were television crews from all the American networks and several foreign ones, reporters from major national newspapers and newsmagazines, sociologists, government officials, and so on. Some came back several times. Later, after war against poverty was formally declared, we talked with college students and others interested in what was happening in the Kentucky mountains. Many people were interested in both poverty and environmental problems. Strip-mining had increased enormously and the damage became more obvious every day. The negative effects of coal mining on the health of coal miners also were becoming more and more obvious. The area's problems were far beyond the capacity of local efforts to solve them. Most of the nation knew little of conditions in Appalachia, so we spent much of our time and energy trying to show people from other parts of the country what things were like here.

We were among the first papers to write about the problems caused by strip-mining, a process by which coal is removed from the tops and sides of mountains instead of from underground. Until the federal government passed laws regulating the process in 1977, mining companies were free to get the coal out any way they wanted and were not required to reclaim the hillsides they had scarred. In the early 1960s, we carried our first photograph showing the effects of strip-mining and we followed and reported the widespread development of citizen protests against coal companies that were destroying people's homes and farms by strip-mining. At that time the landowners were helpless. The coal companies' mineral deeds permitted them to get the coal in whatever way they pleased, and it took a thirty-year effort by many people to get a new law limiting the use of the infamous Kentucky "broad-form deed." Something of a war was fought—sometimes with words, sometimes with guns and dynamite, sometimes with sabotage.

Public outcries against strip-mining practices and against unsafe conditions in eastern Kentucky's deep mines brought more observers into our area, and we continued to serve as tour guides and offer the use of the newspaper office and darkroom as needed. We had one coal-operator friend, but the rest didn't think very highly of us. The largest group of outside reporters to arrive at one time came in response to two explosions that killed twenty-six men at the Scotia mine in Letcher County in March 1976. These twin explosions and the public hearings held afterward brought about the passage of stronger federal mine safety laws.

In the early 1970s, Whitesburg police, joined by sheriff's deputies, confronted young people in the community over such offenses as boys sitting on the railings of a bridge on Main Street in Whitesburg that crosses the Kentucky River, here only two feet deep and twenty feet wide. The boys were charged with whistling at girls and women who passed by and with playing their car radios too loud. Several kids were beaten by law officers in various incidents around the county and some were jailed for questionable reasons. Some youths were shot. The paper detailed it all, and this angered the lawmen.

While this was going on, there developed a situation involving the coal industry and overloaded coal trucks, which were destroying poorly paved mountain roads. Coal operators and truckers met to discuss plans for dodging the problem. One coal operator told the crowd, "If Tom Gish gets word of this and prints anything, we'll burn his paper down." A reporter from the *Louisville Courier-Journal* was present and reported the threat.

During this period we were getting frequent threats against our children, our business, and our home. We told city and county officials about what was happening and asked for help. It became high comedy when we called that ultimate authority, the FBI, and the agent called us back from the Letcher County sheriff's office saying we should ask the sheriff for protection.

A few weeks later the newspaper's office and most of its contents were destroyed in a predawn fire caused by a kerosene firebomb tossed through a window by a youth who was at that time a student in a law-enforcement curriculum at one of Kentucky's universities. A long, painful investigation followed. We found ourselves and our son accused. Eventually, however, state police established that a Whitesburg city policeman, who also was a sheriff's deputy, had hired some boys to burn the newspaper. The policeman and the boys were arrested. Most charges were plea-bargained away, but the policeman was tried by a special commonwealth's attorney who came up from Lexington, and he was convicted by a Letcher Circuit Court jury on a charge of procuring arson. He was sentenced to a two-year prison term, which was probated on condition that he leave the state for those two years.

It appeared that those who plotted the *Eagle* arson hoped to pin it all on police-youth confrontations. But an attorney hired to represent one of the boys told us later that the boys involved had been shown a big roll of bills—he cupped his hands to illustrate—and were told there would be plenty of money for everyone. Everyone knew it was coal money, the attorney remarked.

All these things happened because the *Mountain Eagle* refused to censor itself on issues involving big industry and common people. The coal industry has a long history of telling one and all what to believe and how to vote. Cross it and you're out of a job. Never would it sit still and let some tiny little newspaper challenge total industry control of the land and people of eastern Kentucky.

Here's another example. For the past couple of years the people who live in the Camp Branch and Indian Creek areas of Letcher County have complained that the underground mining going on in their neighborhoods was destroying their wells and their water supplies. We ran several stories about their troubles and reported on a series of local meetings at which state and federal officials talked about the problem. The officials assured the property owners that Golden Oak Mining Company, the coal company responsible for the damage, would have to restore their water supplies. Meanwhile the state ordered the company to pay for filters and other supplies needed as a result of the mining damage. After one of those meetings, Golden Oak distributed letters to its employees accusing "certain people who are not interested in progress . . . along with the *Mountain Eagle* and others" of "making a political football out of Golden Oak's efforts to be a progressive supporter of the community" and of "working against us and our future." In April 1999, nineteen families filed suit against the coal company, demanding that it provide a public water supply to replace the private ones it had destroyed.

A news story that appeared in the fall of 1998 also had an effect on us. Most mountain people can't afford to build or buy a home. Local banks don't want to finance homes except for short periods at high interest rates. Our residents are paying 10 percent interest or more for a ten- or fifteen-year home mortgage, even though branches of the same banking firms make loans available to homebuyers in central Kentucky at 7 percent interest over longer periods. We asked some questions, wrote a story, and printed it on the front page. That produced a result. The bank, which had been an every-week advertiser since the 1930s depression, apparently did not want its high Whitesburg interest rates compared to the sharply lower rates charged in Lexington by its parent bank. The bank canceled all its advertising and told us not to bother trying to sell it ads. It will call us if it ever wants to run another ad.

Should we have been more concerned about the paper's finances and exercised self-censorship, thus not offending the bank? Or were we doing the correct thing when we sought to explain why so few new homes were being built? We made what we thought was the only acceptable choice.

We no longer panic when such things happen. We have developed dozens of smaller advertising accounts from all kinds of locally owned small businesses—used car lots, auto repairmen, beauticians, plumbers, painters, a long list. Since we became owners of the paper, the price per copy has grown from a nickel to seventy-five cents, and the circulation has grown from twenty-one hundred to six thousand. Circulation income now pays our printing and postage bills with some money left over for other expenses.

Our efforts to serve the interests of our readers keep us doing things a lot of papers dropped long ago. Our community correspondents keep readers in the know about who is sick, who has sons and daughters visiting from Ohio, who is on the honor roll at college. Sometimes they throw in their own observations about national and world events, or they criticize local government for icy roads or some other shortcoming. These columns are forums for all kinds of viewpoints. A lot of this we inherited when we bought the paper. But in those early years, we made the stupid mistake of cutting out the opinions. After a lot of reader complaints we backed off and let the correspondents have their say. Instead of columns with label headlines, though, we began to pick out some comment or event and feature that in the headline. It is still not unusual for the *Eagle* to have five-column headlines such as "Sherd Martin Kills 5 Copperheads."

We always try to respond to people who call to ask us to come and take a look at some strip-mining or other environmental damage, or perhaps to come and photograph the big potatoes some gardener has grown. And if a proud parent brings in a photo of a child, we print it. Nothing that comes our way from the community is ignored.

We don't have an obituary column, but we write a small news story when someone dies, and we give each a one- or two-line headline.

One of the most popular things in the *Eagle* is a weekly column called "Speak Your Piece," which allows readers to phone in comments to an answering machine and talk about whatever they want to. We transcribe the messages, edit them for possible libel, and then run them in each week's edition. The subject matter and the ages of the callers cover wide ranges. The column has been in the paper every week since 1983. It generally takes up a page or more of space and it and the television schedule are the most-read parts of the paper. A local public radio station reads items from "Speak Your Piece" on a late-afternoon broadcast every Wednesday. The original idea wasn't ours. We got it from a Michigan newspaper that sold tips for weekly editors. Our version, however, is considerably broader and more political than the original. Some of our newspaper friends think it is wrong to use this kind of thing, but we are convinced that this page gives a voice to people who otherwise would not have one.

We have a list of rules that we guess qualify as self-censorship, but until now we hadn't written them down. Here are some:

We don't use photos of welfare recipients in situations that may be embarrassing to them or to their children.

We straighten up grammar when we are quoting someone. Why embarrass somebody by putting poor grammar into print? It's not the person's fault that he or she doesn't know better, and why should we perpetuate bad grammar when seeing the right way may bring about proper use the next time?

We do not identify suicide as the cause of death except in unusual circumstances, such as the suicide of a prominent public figure.

In cases of deaths that appear in news stories involving crimes, we try also to run a separate notice with just the usual funeral home information in addition to what other coverage may be necessary in a straight news story. Why carry a bad situation into the rest of a family's life when a simple death notice can go into a family's scrapbook instead?

We do not use gory pictures of accidents or crimes.

One problem with being a small-town editor is that as soon as the paper is out, you may walk out the door and run into the guy you mentioned unfavorably in an editorial or someone involved in some questionable activity that you reported. This you learn to accept. But it's a little harder for your five kids when their best friends may be the children of someone you have taken to task. One of our daughters came home in terror from a visit to a friend because she had been at the family's dinner table when the talk turned to something that had been in the *Eagle,* and an adult guest commented that people would "just have to burn the *Eagle* down if it keeps on like that." That incident occurred fifteen years before somebody finally did set fire to the paper. Also, a high school teacher made unfavorable comments about the paper before a class that included one of our sons. And our children can recall times when mothers of their school friends obviously didn't want their kids associating with ours.

In the early years what we wrote sometimes made other members of our family who also lived in Letcher County uncomfortable. They would sometimes ask why we wrote something, but even if they disagreed with us, they supported our right to print what we thought.

There's a lot of discussion these days as to whether it's proper for newspaper editors to take an active as well as an opinionated part in the development of their communities. Some people think the role of the press is to observe and comment and not to drive outsiders around explaining local conditions and problems to them. We decided early that we had to take an active role in bringing the problems of eastern Kentucky and Letcher County to the attention of those who might help, whether they were students, political scientists, industrialists, government officials, or whatever. We're still doing it. We also were determined to give our mountain readers the facts and information needed to help them confront their many problems. We're still doing that, too.

Our paper's reporting was not welcomed by subscribers or public officials forty years ago. Today we get loud complaints if we fail to attend meetings and report what happens, and most public officials accept our presence. We still think we have the best job in the country. And we still have not learned how to report happy news.

2.

The Corporate Domination of Journalism

By Ronnie Dugger

As founding editor of the Texas Observer, *an independent weekly newspaper noted for its irreverence, its bite and wit, and its wide-ranging journalistic excellence, Ronnie Dugger made something of a habit of printing stories that reporters felt they could not get printed elsewhere. The* Observer *quickly became known for its muckraking—a lovely old term—and Dugger and his staff exposed corruption among legislators and lobbyists, poor conditions in state reform schools and mental hospitals, tax dodging and environmental pollution by Texas oil companies, and issues of racial injustice and civil liberties violations. Among his contributors, and allies, were Willie Morris, Molly Ivins, Robert Sherrill, and Larry King.*

Dugger began in newspapers at age thirteen, when he became a copyboy at the San Antonio Express-News. *While at the University of Texas he covered the state legislature for the* Daily Texan, *the student newspaper. He studied at Oxford University, then, with the backing of a group of liberal Democrats, began the* Observer *upon his return to Texas. He was publisher of the paper from 1967 until June 1994, when it was turned into a nonprofit foundation.*

Dugger is a prolific newspaper and magazine writer and

essayist, and now a full-time author. His books include On Reagan: The Man and His Presidency; The Politician: The Life and Times of Lyndon Johnson; *and* Our Invaded Universities: Form, Reform and New Starts. *"One of my goals," Dugger said, "has been to keep control of what subjects I work on, and, with exceptions necessary to survive financially, I have done so." With the spread of corporate control of the media, he fears that his kind of journalistic independence has just about disappeared.*

When I started out as a boy in journalism in Texas fifty-six years ago, most reporters were channeled, by the well-understood configurations of the local powers, into an undescribed, silently enforced conspiracy. "Don't break the moral silence"—that was the gist of it. Most reporters censored themselves when they decided what to report and what not to. Slums in the late-afternoon shadows of the state capitol? Skip it. A Mexican guy in a West Texas jail for one hundred years for fondling one marijuana cigarette? Two paragraphs. White boys joyriding down back roads in East Texas, shooting black schoolchildren who were dancing, killing a boy, age eleven? Three paragraphs. A new naturopathy bill provided to its legislative sponsor in two copies, with five hundred dollars attached? You can't prove that, boy.

The news, young fellow, the old editor would say, is

the candidates' speeches, the mayor's budget, the crime, the weather, the business news from local companies. A rare rebel reporter or two—Robert Sherrill of the *Austin American-Statesman,* Ernest Bailey of the *Houston Press,* then the *El Paso Herald-Post*—proved that if you had the guts you could report the facts of racial prejudice, brutal official state neglect of the poor, the corruption of legislators by business interests. But Robert and Ernest stood out like foolhardy giants.

In 1954 in Austin a group of Texas liberals started up a weekly newspaper of reportage and dissent, the *Texas Observer.* When I reported in it the nightrider shootings of the black schoolkids in East Texas, the FBI came into the case, the local district attorney accused me of suppressing evidence even though I had identified the killers as suspects to a deputy sheriff, and the killers were at least convicted and got Deep South justice: five years, suspended.

When I put out a special issue of the *Observer* on the lobbyists in the legislature, I included in it one long section headed "They Talk of Bribery," in which I quoted senators or representatives, but without their names, telling about bribes among their number. I had simply promised each member who told one of the chilling stories that I would go to jail rather than identify him or her. I went down to the capitol the afternoon the issue reached the legislators' offices and saw members swiveled back at their seats in both the House and Senate reading it in deep concentration, most of them knowing, of course, about some of the cases reported.

Where were the reporters on the dailies? They were minding their p's, for promotions, and q's, for careers. Some of them, working, for example, for the *Dallas Morning News* of that day, were shameless. I learned, as any hardworking reporter could have, that the chairman of the Texas Railroad Commission, which despite its name supposedly regulated the oil industry in the name of and on behalf of the Great State of Texas, was personally profiting from farm-out drilling contracts from the major oil companies. I blasted this story, including the commissioner's copious admissions and explanations, across the front page of the *Observer.* Maybe we only had six thousand subscribers, but we did have six thousand. It was as if we had none. There was a total silence about this scandal, and about the commissioner's admissions and explanations, in the entire daily and broadcast press of Texas. Being a traditionally tough investigative reporter in Texas in the 1950s was like playing your guitar without hearing anything. About a year later the *Dallas News,* making no mention of my story, as if breaking the news for the first time, reported that—Wow!—the chairman of the railroad commission was taking farm-outs from the major oil companies he was regulating. It never occurred to me to protest. It was as if one had disappeared without being killed. Maybe I was imagining it all.

Now an effigy of any newspaper that did to that

story of mine what the *Dallas News* did would be strung from the lamppost at Main and Broadway in a dozen towns in Texas at high noon. The daily newspapers of Texas are better professionally now, coverage is more balanced, and the *Dallas News* has international coverage that competes respectably with that of the nation's four great newspapers, which in my opinion are the *New York Times,* the *Washington Post,* the *Wall Street Journal,* and the *Los Angeles Times.* Still, there is a frightening difference between then and now.

Reporters then knew that management might kill stories or put in editors who wouldn't permit stories the boss wouldn't like. But they also knew, and knew correctly, that their papers would usually stand behind them and that there were enough independently owned newspapers that sooner or later glimmerings of even the most censorable stories had a fair chance of getting into print. Somebody somewhere and their editor wouldn't censor it, or at least not completely. Reporters were still professionals in a profession and they worked for bosses who were people.

One has to shuffle a hatful of phrases and pluck out one to try to describe the difference now in a few words. For the time being, domination of journalism by large corporations will have to do. Essentially, in the mainstream media in which prevailing public opinion is shaped and formed, freedom of the press has been transformed into a special-interest shield wielded by the major so-called media corporations, which are actually advertising and entertainment corporations. Freedom of the press, which was meant to protect freedom of speech, instead protects big corporations' selling for profit. Ideas and thoughts and moods that lead people into brainless twittering and endless buying predominate in what has become our common social context.

The newspapers and radio and television stations have been bought up and linked together into a few powerful conglomerates. The NBC network is owned by General Electric, the largest industrial conglomerate in the world, with interests in almost everything. Each of these clanking chains and rankling networks is run by one man, the reigning corporate CEO, for a few controlling owners, and these few corporate monarchs set the pervading tones and agendas for us all. Freedom of the press has turned out to mean, in the real world, control of the mainstream press by a small number of oligarchs. Freedom of the press has been upside-downed into corporate control of the press, which is no more freedom of the press than government control is. Freedom of the press, far from guaranteeing democracy—its purpose when the country was founded—now protects the corporations that are methodically debasing democracy.

Corporate censorship now shapes the whole mainstream media process. With the abundance of media owners replaced by a few media conglomerates, corporate censorship can and with increasing strength does determine and control both the content and the direction of the national life. The self-censorship exercised by a reporter in 1949, detouring around blatant injustice because he's thinking about shoes for his kids and doesn't want to get fired, was nothing compared to the corporate censorship of today. If those were the days, these are the nights.

The reporter, for the dissemination of whose honest work the press is supposed to be free, is subordinated now to the nature of the corporation itself and to the mass-audience requirements, ideological restraints, profit-making imperatives, and preferences for a quiescent and obediently buying population of those same advertising and entertainment corporations. Freedom of the press now conceals and, by the workings of perverted constitutional law, protects corporate control of the press. Journalism has become the captive of advertising and entertainment corporations. Even as our nation of reasonably competitive free enterprise and democracy has become instead a nation dominated by major corporations that control politics as well as economics, the corporate conglomerates have transformed journalism into corporate moneymaking while falsely claiming that it's still journalism.

We are so immersed and passively involved in "the media," we are so checkmated by entrenched corporate seizures of the First Amendment, that we do not see the mortal threat to democracy that the corporate domination of the press is, and even when we glimpse the specter in the shadows we don't believe we can do anything about it. We believe in freedom of the press so much that we let the media monopolists silence us by chanting "freedom of the press" as they strangle it.

The corporate domination of the mainstream media is masking the thwarting of our democracy that is now occurring in all of its major venues. X-raying and democratizing those media is the most necessary single project confronting us as citizens. For those citizens who are journalists, the challenge is to turn away from submission as professionals to corporate domination; the work ahead is to revive old or devise new mainstream institutions within which we can freely serve the public's right and need to be honestly informed on everything that we as working journalist-citizens think matters.

Let's test the present against a ringing principle, one enunciated by Lawrence Grossman, the former president of NBC News and of PBS: "No government or small group of big corporations should ever be permitted to control the majority, or even a large proportion, of our vital sources of information."

The presidential dereliction and congressional collapses that permitted the profession of journalism to be enclosed and subdued by a small group of big corporations are not hard to find. In 1969 a corrupt bargain was struck between seven newspaper chains and President Nixon: You support our bill and we'll support your reelection. The bill that became law as a result of the deal was the Newspaper Preservation Act, which exempted the monopolization of the daily newspapers in a single city from antitrust laws. Consequently, most city daily newspapers are monopolies.

A quarter century later, Congress in practical effect repealed the antitrust laws for radio and television in the Telecommunications Act of 1996, perhaps the largest giveaway of public property in American history. As a result of that law, each license-holder of a television channel now has the use and control of six or more channels—still free of any payment to we the people who own those channels. Instead of diversifying the use of channels that were multiplied six- or more-fold by advances in technology, Congress, by this act, knowingly and therefore criminally magnified the power of the existing media oligarchy. Republican Bob Dole, the leader of his party in the Senate when the law passed, said it was a giveaway of federal property worth as much as seventy billion dollars.

"Before the Act," according to Reed Hundt, chairman of the Federal Communications Commission when the act passed, "a radio group could own only forty stations nationally and two in any single market; now it can own more than 1,000, including multiple stations within individual markets." In fact, under the law one company can now own every radio station in the country, and one company can own up to 35 percent of all American television stations. In any single city one company can own newspapers, radio stations, and television stations.

The 1996 giveaway was justified by Congress, and by President Clinton as he signed it, in the name of competition. In the first three years after the act passed, the merger deals in telecommunications had a value of far more than one hundred billion dollars. Cable rates, far from falling, rose.

In the United States, big corporations—and therefore the few people who are their CEOs—control the major media: television, radio, the major newspapers and magazines, and the major book publishers and booksellers. That means that these few men:

- control much of the access to our minds and the selection of what we are invited to think about;
- use the airways that we the people own free of any payment to us to propagandize us and to enrich themselves and their corporations at profit rates that media mogul Barry Diller says are as high as 30 to 60 percent a year if you've got brain one;
- expose the typical seven-year-old child to twenty thousand commercials a year;
- and teach us crime and violence, and violence and crime, and crime and violence, to sell us products.

On the average an American child spends 900 hours a year in school, but 1,500 hours a year watching TV.

What is the new "school" teaching? Before your or my children or grandchildren are out of grade school, they will witness an average of 8,000 murders and 100,000 additional acts of violence. Then the child is ready for junior high.

In North America there are about 1,800 daily papers, 11,000 magazines, 2,000 TV stations, 11,000 radio stations, 3,000 book publishers, and 7 major movie studios. That's real diversity, right? I'm afraid not. In 1983 in each of these media, forty-six corporations owned and controlled more than 50 percent of the business. Nine years later that number had shrunk to twenty controlling corporations—that is, twenty controlling CEOs.

In those same nine years, the number of companies controlling more than half of the national daily newspaper circulation dropped from twenty to eleven; controlling more than half of total magazine revenues, from twenty to two; controlling more than half of book-publishing revenues, from eleven to five. "As a result," Ben Bagdikian, the media critic, wrote, "The same few firms are slowly tightening their stranglehold on the news, views, literature, and entertainment that reach a majority of Americans."

In 1945 about 80 percent of U.S. daily newspapers were independently owned. By 1989, about 80 percent were owned by corporate chains. Upside-down.

And for the most part the links these chains were adding were local monopolies.

Huge corporations own the four major U.S. television networks and unmistakably those corporations now run the networks' news divisions, too. The commercial networks, including their news divisions, have abandoned all but the simulation of public service. Walter Cronkite said, "People come to me all the time now and say, 'I can't get any news on the air any more.' . . . Television today . . . foreshortens reporting. . . . And then it goes for tabloid junk—Hollywood personalities and crime stories. We're shirking our responsibility as broadcasters." Dan Rather agreed: "The Hollywoodization of the news is deep and abiding. . . . We run stupid celebrity stories. . . ."

Public funding for public TV and radio has been skimped by the Congress—itself dominated by the large corporations just as journalism is—and this has required public radio and TV to get commercial corporate advertising to keep going. Predictably, indeed intentionally, that has corroded the independence and the quality of public TV and radio.

It's well said that "Control of information is political power." The press, Theodore White once wrote, "sets the agenda for public discussion" and "determines what people think about and write about." With control of mass-media technology, the CEOs who run the advertising and entertainment empires can proliferate their messages hundreds of thousands, millions, tens of millions of times a day.

"It is normal," Bagdikian wrote, "for all large businesses to make serious efforts to influence the news, to avoid bad publicity, and to maximize sympathetic public opinion and government policies. Now they own most of the news media that they wish to influence." This amounts to the ascension of major media owners and CEOs to more and more power over opinion, politics, economics, culture, and society—in short, over the shape, texture, direction, and content of our lives.

What are these companies whose CEOs control public education and public imagination? Time Warner is the biggest media company in the world. Among the other twenty are Disney, Westinghouse, General Electric, Dow Jones, Hearst, Newhouse, Rupert Murdoch's News Corporation, and Paramount.

Bagdikian clinched the point. "Modern technology and American economics have," he wrote, "quietly created a new kind of central authority over information—the national and multinational corporation." In North America, twenty corporate CEOs "constitute a new Private Ministry of Information and Culture."

Around the world, the means for the mass dissemination of expression are being gobbled up by these media-wielding conglomerates. There's never been anything like it. Through their possession of modern communications technology, these gigantic corporations have taken control of the current affairs, entertainment, and cultural content of the human race. The replacement of the hegemony of government by the hegemony of the private corporation is being consolidated by the advertising and entertainment (or, if you prefer, the media) corporations.

A corporation's journalistic employees, its reporters, columnists, editorial writers, news writers, correspondents, and announcers, may seek to exercise their personal First Amendment rights by employing the corporation's means for the dissemination of expression. But since 1886 the Supreme Court has given corporations all the constitutional rights of persons except the Fifth Amendment and the right to vote. A corporation's decision not to disseminate its employees' expression is the use of corporate power against both free speech and freedom of the press, but the federal judiciary says that this is not unconstitutional or illegal, it is just the corporation's exercise of *its* rights of free speech and press.

Freedom of expression is not just for publishers and not just for the press; manifestly, it is for every citizen. Since there is no inherent right to have one's expression disseminated by another, how can the interests of the receivers of communication be protected from censorship by the advertising, entertainment, and industrial conglomerates that control the media mainstream?

A second great but neglected question about freedom of expression concerns its ability to reach receivers of communications. In this respect, Ralph Nader, the consumer advocate, contrasted the early days of the republic to the present. For citizens gathered at the town square in the early days, freedom of expression was relatively equal because it depended on the reach of one's voice. Nowadays there is what Nader called "the decibel problem," the concentrated ownership of the technology for disseminating expression that enables a few wealthy, powerful persons to amplify their messages millions, even billions of times.

A few persons have now acquired what may already be, and—assuming the continuation of present patterns and trends—will certainly become, control of the dominating reach of expression among the majority of the people in the United States and the world.

What so far are the principal consequences of the domination of mainstream journalism by the large advertising and entertainment corporations?

The definition of news has been debased. Bent on getting the highest Nielsen ratings, the network newscasts are lightweight, jump-about, sensationalist, given over to self-help and sentimentality. Local TV news is crime, disasters, sports, the weather. According to *Editor and Publisher*, 48 percent of newspaper editors and publishers polled say that newspaper news coverage is shallow and inadequate, and still they produce it. Television sports are the news opiate of the masses, shilled by the sport-glorifying, hero-building game callers.

Magazines, the *New York Times* reported, are becoming "intimate marketing partners" with advertisers—that is, they are going into business with their advertisers, producing special issues, sponsoring joint events.

American elections have been trumped as thoughtful exercises in citizen education by the cost of radio and television time for political candidates. The candidates who can get enough money from the big corporations and very wealthy donors get the time on the radio and TV channels that we own to sell themselves to us or to blight their opponents. This is not a system for the facilitation of democratic campaigns; this is a system for the destruction of democracy.

Owners and their appointed agents select the anchors, commentators, and itinerant pundits who will cross-examine, on such mass venues as *Nightline* or the Sunday talk shows, the nation's leaders and their policies, while these anchors, commentators, and pundits project their own attitudes and opinions to the millions of citizens watching national TV. The major media owners and their CEOs are the unelected powers behind these talking heads on the publicly owned airways.

Generally speaking, corporate domination of journalism has accelerated the weakening of labor unions in the United States. The corporations that now control our mass media glorify business and the corporation while virtually ignoring ordinary working people. Quick: name one daily newspaper that does not have a business section. No? Then name one daily newspaper that does have a labor section. No? Can you recall daily newspapers supporting a workers' strike or higher wages for them? Probably not. Most major corporations are run by rich men who are antiunion. The half million youngsters who currently deliver newspapers to homes are treated as independent contractors, with no workers' benefits. Fourteen hundred workers who struck the Detroit dailies were locked out.

Corporate censorship happens. In his fourth edition of *Media Monopoly*, Bagdikian reported that the CEO of General Electric told the head of NBC News during the 1987 stock crash not to use wordings in news reports that might hurt GE stock; that the *Dallas Morning News* fired a reporter because a story of his offended an Abilene bank; that McGraw-Hill recalled all copies of a book at the behest of British Petroleum; that Exxon and Mobil pressured United Press International to take a certain reporter off stories about oil and taxes. Disney CEO Michael Eisner was quoted in *Brill's Content* as saying, "ABC News knows that I would prefer them not to cover [Disney]." Archer Daniels Midland's underwriting of the

Public Broadcasting System's *Newshour* in 1995 apparently compromised the program's coverage when ADM was accused of price-fixing. ABC Radio dropped populist Jim Hightower's national commentary show, which had two million listeners, as soon as it became known that Eisner would take over Disney/ABC, either because Hightower had said on the air that now he would be working for a mouse—or because, as ABC said, he did not have enough listeners and advertisers.

We may also be seeing a new pattern emerging, the corporation versus the reporter. In each case the question turns on disputed stories, so each case requires a separate evaluation that I do not here undertake. But the questions raised are troubling.

The *San Jose Mercury News* turned on reporter Gary Webb when the CIA denied Webb's series about a "dark alliance" between the CIA, the Nicauraguan contras, and drug smugglers. Webb was forced out of his job. The CIA now acknowledges that, as the *New York Times* reported, the agency "continued to work with about two dozen Nicaragua rebels and their supporters during the 1980s despite allegations that they were trafficking in drugs," and the CIA admits doing in effect nothing about many reports it received that the U.S.-financed contras were smuggling drugs into the United States.

An investigative series ran in the *Cincinnati Enquirer* on the business practices of a hometown company, Chiquita Brands International. On grounds that one of the reporters on the story had stolen the company's voice mail, the *Enquirer* repudiated the series and paid the company ten million dollars. The reporter betrayed his source; both have been sentenced to terms of years in prison, suspended.

The show *60 Minutes* stood down to the legal department of CBS and shelved an interview with a tobacco whistle-blower. CNN retracted its report that U.S. forces used nerve gas during the Vietnam War.

Monsanto, top officials of Rupert Murdoch's Fox network, and the Fox affiliate WTVT-TV in Tampa, Florida, engaged in a yearlong dispute with the station's two investigative reporters about their reporting concerning Monsanto's rGBH growth hormone, which is fed to cows, increases their milk production, makes some of them sick, and is linked in some studies to cancer in humans. The trouble started after Monsanto sent a letter to the president of Fox News challenging the story. The reporters, Jane Akre and Steve Wilson, were asked to rewrite their script more than seventy times. Their corporate superiors said no to every version. Akre and Wilson quoted one station official as telling them that Fox had paid three billion dollars for that station and its executives would decide what the news was. Finally the reporters were released from their contracts and the story was killed. Akre and Wilson told me that the station offered them two hundred thousand dollars in severance pay if they would pledge to keep quiet about the whole thing.

They refused the money, sued the station, and posted all their reports, evidence, and sources on a website.

A free press—honest, tough reporters—can keep any government or business honest. Daniel Ellsberg stole the Pentagon Papers but great newspapers ran with the story. The Watergate reporting brought down President Nixon. Investigative journalism, national, state, and local, often stops wrongdoing and sets things right. Journalism that works is essential to democracy. The news side of the *Journal,* the *Times* on each coast, and the *Post* are four of the most important battalions for democracy and justice.

Integrity persists not only in the profession but also among some of the corporations that enclose it. The four-part special investigative series on corporate welfare costs in *Time* magazine in 1998, written by Donald L. Bartlett and James B. Steele, is a stellar example of this. And reporters give people in democracies the only reliable direct information they get on their governments' wars and foreign policies. Just think of the indispensable role of reporters, risking their lives along with everyone else, in Vietnam and in Kosovo.

But on behalf of democracy, which depends on the knowledge of the whole people serviced by the media (which now are captives of corporate conglomerates), we must keep in mind how the structure of corporate journalism works. The owner of the corporation appoints the CEO who appoints the managers who appoint the editors. Those editors—dependent, through the intermediate executives, on the pleasure of the owner and the CEO—hire and fire the reporters and decide what stories the reporters are assigned to write, what stories they are not assigned to write, what the stories that are published say and how they say it, and what stories get killed. Reporters write the stories that run, and all credit and glory go to them for the great stories. But the profit-driven and usually ideologically predictable major owners and CEOs of the corporation, not the journalists, control the media. The corporation, a top-down hierarchy, has the freedom of the press. Property rights trump journalism. As freedom of expression is applied in business and corporate contexts and interpreted by the federal courts, a person's decision to express something is subordinated to a company's decision on what expression to disseminate. Federal judges have validated the corporation's denial of freedom of expression to the journalists who work for the corporation.

If, as I for one believe, not just the press but democracy is at stake, journalists and citizens and journalists as citizens must challenge the constitutionality of corporate journalism.

It is easy to come up with a list of proposed reforms that, if enacted by the Congress, would restore democratic values and establish democratic structure for our newspapers, radio, and television. Repeal the scandalous 1969 and 1996 laws that exempt the mass media from the antitrust laws. Abolish the one-paper local monopolies. Enact stiff low limits on how many media entities, of what kinds, in what locations, any one owner may have, and phase out the advertising and entertainment media giants by mandated divestitures. Abolish the cable oligopolies so these five hundred distinctive cable stations we were promised can exist independently. Tax commercial advertising 5 percent to 7 percent to generate seven billion to ten billion dollars a year to reduce the amount of advertising and finance a robust national public radio, television, cybernetic, and cultural and educational network. Or, as the owners of the airways, take for the public treasury 25 percent of the radio and TV licensees' income and use it to fund the public sphere, including earmarked subsidies for categories of cable stations, such as free-speech stations and stations for community organizations and advocacy groups deemed especially valuable for the public good. Ban commercials from programs for children. Reinstate the fairness doctrine and minimums for news and public-service programming. Revoke the licenses of commercial stations in violation. Provide free TV and radio time for ballot-qualified candidates.

But what such a laundry list leaves out is the fact that Congress and the president are now so beholden to wealthy individual and corporate campaign contributors, and elected politicians are so terrified of being either slammed or ignored by their powerful local newspapers or TV stations, that there is no chance they will enact such reforms. Under President Reagan, the fairness doctrine was abolished, so now if you are attacked on the mass broadcast media you have no assured right of reply. Ralph Nader practically had to blow the dome off the Capitol to get a House hearing for his proposal for "audience networks" of listeners and viewers who would determine, by democratic processes, the network programming they watch for one hour a day. Not one congressman, not one, would sponsor the bill.

Professor Robert K. McChesney of the University of Illinois pointed out that in the Progressive era John Dewey and others proposed one remedy that might not require congressional action and would seem not to pose constitutional difficulties: the establishment of newspapers as nonprofit and noncommercial enterprises supported by endowments, with their officers directly elected by the voters or else by the staff at the newspapers.

Serious independent-minded reporters and editors, regardless of their politics, might well form a cooperative of independent journalists whose members, at different levels, would own and control their own media, and who at corporations would form independent journalistic co-ops, unions, or guilds that would undertake to control the hiring and firing and all editorial policies at the corporate news divisions. Who has freedom of the press, people or corporations? Let the judges answer that question, properly put. With the help of constitutional lawyers or constitutional amendments, journalists need to go into unions, or maybe all the way back to medieval guilds, to fight back the corporate profiteers, just as physicians are trying to form unions and associations to fight the for-profit medical corporations.

With ballot initiatives affording state-level activist groups opportunities to propose novel reforms, perhaps local revolts against the central-point media could be sheltered in local institutions. Jerold Starr, a sociology professor at West Virginia University, has been working on ways that local citizens can take a measure of democratic control over the performance of their local broadcast media. Local cable contracts are subject to local political action. Why not, by analogy with local transportation, water, navigation, and power districts, establish local communications districts with taxing powers that would democratically fund local media and try to protect the rights, within their jurisdictions, of the originators of free expression and the receivers of it—persons who read, see, and hear it.

In the scattered domains of lower-circulation,

lower-wattage alternative journalism, there are six alternative news services. There are also the Association of Alternative Newsweeklies, the Pacifica Network, the National Association of Community Broadcasters, National Native News, the National Radio Project, the Prison Radio Project, Radio for Peace International, Radio Nation, and We the People, as well as the stand-alone local periodicals and better-known state and national journals of opinion. The powerful possibility inherent in all this might be a single interactive alternative multimedia system composed of these various autonomous undertakings. Such an emergence could not rival the present commercialized mainstream media, but through systematic sharing, the quality of alternative journalism would improve and its influence grow.

Hope for fundamental legislative reform of the social structure of media lies, in my opinion, in two other directions.

McChesney, the Wisconsin professor, and Lawrence Grossman, formerly of NBC and PBS, postulate a vision of a revived public communications sphere that would exceed in magnitude and import anything that now exists in any country.

"We need public service broadcasting more than ever before," McChesney said in a 1997 paper. "We should think in terms of well-subsidized national services as well as localized public access channels . . . an extraordinary public broadcasting system. . . .

The ultimate goal must be to have the public service sector be the *dominant* component of the broadcasting and media system. Hence the struggle for public service broadcasting cannot avoid direct confrontation and conflict with the existing corporate media giants. Our goal must be to break them up into smaller units, and to encourage the success of media workers' unions as a counterbalance to corporate muscle." [Emphasis in original.] During an interview McChesney added, "We need a system that is not controlled from any one source, not by one person or by one institution."

Grossman visualized a new model of a nonprofit national and local telecommunications information consortium. For precedent he cites the land grant act of the last century, under which the nation sold public lands to pay for public universities in the states. "We have some extraordinary and highly respected information-providing institutions already in existence, our public library systems, our great research universities, our museums and science institutions," Grossman said. Along with the public broadcasters, these institutions would provide education, job retraining, public health education, and other such continuing education services; publicly relevant information on the important issues; documentaries, public discussions, electronic town meetings, free political airtime; attention to high-quality and local culture and arts, particularly original material; and programming for children, all of this abetted with printouts, textbooks, courses, help, and information on request. It would be, Grossman said, "a kind of retail, electronic Library of Congress, if you will, that is to serve all of the people, all of the time."

McChesney called for the injection of media reform and a new vision of the public sphere into the public debates fostered by new-line political entities. He directed attention to bold media-reform platforms among new-line political parties in many countries abroad: the Alliance in New Zealand, to roll back corporate control of the media; the New Democratic Party in Canada, to break up Canadian corporate media chains and expand the public network; the Left Party in Sweden, to abolish all advertising on radio and TV and to subsidize a diverse range of viewpoints in the print media; and the Workers Party in Brazil, staging mass protests outside broadcast companies with policies they object to.

Media issues are not now part of American campaign debates and party platforms. In our country, as McChesney said, "Our most immediate job is to put media issues on the political agenda, to convince people that it is their right in a democratic society to establish a media system that serves their needs."

In parallel course or in due course, the historic absurdity of corporate personhood, which makes the corporation the Supercitizen and the rest of us Subcitizens, will have to be dealt with if democracy is to continue. For our purposes here it is enough to realize that we have let the corporations, their lawyers, and the federal judges steal freedom of the press from the people and lodge it in the corporations.

"What is most striking about the existing corporate media system," McChesney said, "is how absurd it really is. We have the technology and the resources to establish an extraordinarily rich and diverse media system. . . . In the end, our goal should be not merely to have a series of national media systems with dominant public service components, but to have a global public sphere as well."

A mainstream media that is public broadcasting. A nonprofit national and local education and information consortium of our public broadcasters, libraries, universities, museums, and the Internet. Finally, a global public sphere. In the civilly holy causes of freedom of the press and freedom of expression, a public alternative to the corporate mainstream media can be visualized and demanded.

3.

Excuses, Excuses

How Editors and Reporters Justify Ignoring Stories

By E. R. Shipp

Although censorship by people outside the newsroom, be it government, advertisers, or corporate owners, is the kind of censorship most reporters think of first, any honest examination of the issue makes clear that there are pressures within the newsroom as well. Sometimes they come from the reporter's ambitions, sometimes from political jockeying among editors, sometimes from the editors' definition of news.

E. R. Shipp, now the ombudsman, or readers' advocate, for the Washington Post, *has seen these pressures. Shipp was a reporter covering legal affairs for the* New York Times, *then a columnist for the* New York Daily News, *where she won the 1995 Pulitzer Prize for commentary. She is also on the faculty of the Columbia University Graduate School of Journalism.*

When we think of censorship, we usually think in terms of what government does in muzzling, or trying to muzzle, a free press. Sometimes, particularly in a world in which conglomerates are gobbling up what for them are mere assets, but which frequently include newspapers and television stations among the widgets, we think of corporate America muzzling, or potentially muzzling, a free press. And when we think in such terms, whether government is Godzilla or corporate America is the culprit, we are righteously indignant, and not a little afraid. After all, we are guardians of democracy—sentries with pens, notebooks, computers, and, much more important than these tools, words.

I came into this business some twenty years ago, with a passion to tell stories, to be a voice for the voiceless, to build bridges between people who think they have nothing in common but enmity, to right wrongs, to fight the good fights. My passion was still intact when I joined the staff of the *New York Times* in January 1980, as green but as cocky as they came.

Some reporters begin to feel the passion seep right away when they are placed on general assignment in the newsroom of a newspaper as large and, at least back then, as impersonal as the *Times* could be. If you started your shift at 11 A.M., then you would pick up the scraps that the beat reporters hadn't already pounced on or that the editors wanted their star—or, at least, more senior—reporters to have. I have seen new reporters struggling to find something to sink their teeth into, to attract the attention of the editors who matter, to win their confidence. And I have seen many fail and give up. If they value the prestige of saying that they work at such a newspaper, they may just settle in, do piddling stories, and never, ever rock the boat.

Perhaps I was too stupid to realize that some of the assignments I got in my first days at the *Times* were losers as far as the assigning editor was concerned. But I took a few lemons and made some pretty good lemonade. Mark Twain fans on the anniversary of his death. Musicians' union fight. Heroes honored by the New York Police Department. All the while I was doing these metro front, or "B1," stories, I was looking for those that I could tell, that I had come to the *Times* to tell, stories that involved the law. Early on I found a pretty good one: a threatened strike by the transit union that would directly challenge the Taylor Law, which forbade strikes by public employees. Some editors wondered if I was ready to do an analysis of such an important law. But I did it.

I came to the paper with all sorts of ideas about stories I wanted to work on, but I had one rule that still pains me when I think of the stories that might have gotten into the *Times* in my first three years on staff. That rule was this: I would not volunteer to do black stories, stories about Harlem and Bedford-Stuyvesant, about gangs and dysfunctional families, about long hot summers to be or neighborhoods that once were something before the blacks and browns moved in. I lived in Harlem. But I did not want to become the Harlem correspondent. They had hired me at the *Times* largely because of my background in law, they said to me—and I took them at and held them to their word. Because they had recently settled a discrimination lawsuit brought by women of the *Times* and because they were in the midst of discrimination litigation brought by the nonwhites, they might have been more impressed by my gender and my race than by my academic degrees. But they didn't say that to me.

Thus, for me, self-censorship was a consequence of personal pride and ambition to get ahead rather than be stuck in the job of "urban affairs reporter" or "civil rights reporter" or "race relations reporter" or other such nomenclature for a position that meant little until riot time or a bloodletting within the leadership ranks of the NAACP. My goal was to write about legal matters. When I came upon stories—and I did at least several times a week just by going to church, shopping in the local inadequate grocery stores, hanging out at a neighborhood restaurant called The Red Rooster that was frequented by Harlem's movers and shakers, or walking to and from the subway on Lenox Avenue—I would not volunteer to do them, but I would send notes to the appropriate reporters. Something afoot at Harlem Hospital? I might tell the health reporter. Something going down between rival political factions? I might tell the political boys and girls. A scandal in one of the major churches? I'd tell the religion reporters or the writers of the People column, as the paper's rather highbrow gossip column was called back when. Most of the time my tips were ignored. The stories went untold.

My first beat was covering the justice system. Predecessors had called it the court beat in Manhattan, but I added to it the city and state courts and the district attorney's office, the Legal Aid Society, the Judicial Conduct Commission, and any and everything related to the quality of justice meted out in New York. In that beat I soon learned that *Times* editors were not interested in most of what went on day-to-day, the run-of-the-mill muggings and rapes and robberies and murders above 110th Street. So I could beat my head against a wall to persuade them to run a news brief or two, or I could set out to look for stories that were more likely to be of interest to them, stories about the system, about the process. Even that was difficult, and, without the rookie's passion that I still had, I might have given up.

I came across the case of a crooked lawyer who had ripped off an elderly woman who had entrusted to him her bank books with the instruction that he pay her monthly household bills, Con Ed, the phone, and so forth. No more than a couple of hundred dollars a month. The lawyer promptly stole thousands of dollars from her for expensive purchases for his wife and himself. The elderly woman—she was about eighty-nine—was being dragged to the court time and again for one pretrial hearing after another. His goal was to wear her down; he hoped that she would expire before trial. I thought this was a good story, so I told my editors that I wanted to cover the trial of a lawyer charged with stealing from an elderly woman. The editor was not interested. The woman was not well known, to him or other editors, and the amount of money was not all that significant—only, as I recall, a couple of hundred thousand dollars. Yes, there was an elitism run amok on that desk. But I wanted to do the story and I had to figure out how to do it. So, I thought: *trend!* In talking to prosecutors and a few candid defense lawyers, I learned that defense lawyers often did what they could to undermine the credibility of elderly crime victims. I put together anecdotal information, talked to the cops about the number of crimes against the elderly, talked to prosecutors about the acquittal rates for defendants charged with victimizing the elderly, looked at the growing number of elderly in New York City, and pitched my story. Of course, the centerpiece of that story was the trial of the lawyer who'd ripped off his elderly client. The story was on the front page. But it came dangerously close to never being told at all.

Here's another example. I knew from friends from law school and others that Haitians who had sought asylum in the United States were being railroaded by the Reagan administration. But a federal court had ruled that they could not be deported without due process, which meant hearings before the Immigration and Naturalization Service. The "usual suspects," one might say, among the left-wing, progressive, and radical lawyers scrambled to represent them. When I proposed doing a story about this effort, all I got was a ho-hum response from the metro desk. But I pressed on, and hit pay dirt. I learned that some of the so-called "white shoe" law firms, the big Wall Street–type law firms, were taking on some of these cases on a pro bono basis. That means they were volunteering to represent the Haitians. Once I could turn this story into one that said more or less, "Wow, Wall Street is challenging Reagan by representing the Haitians," while still focusing on the efforts of the real human rights professionals, the *Times* bit. But that story also came dangerously close to never being told at all.

Through trial and error, I learned to manipulate the system so that stories I wanted to get into the paper and to be handled by a certain editor would not land too soon or too late. For a time at the *Times,* the metropolitan editor and his deputy did not get along, hardly even spoke, and tried their best to undermine each other. Somewhat fortuitously I discovered that this was going on and learned to make sure that an assistant editor who had the ear of the metro editor would pitch my stories. After a run of good page one and metro front pieces, a veteran reporter asked me what the trick was because he was dealing with the deputy and wasn't getting anything into the paper with any kind of prominence. I passed along what I had discovered. These are the games you sometimes have to play, or to make it sound more sophisticated, the strategies you have to adopt, to get your stories into the paper.

What happens when you are just tired of this? That's when you leave or decide, pride be damned, to collect the paycheck and never suggest anything that is complicated or controversial or that will require you to give up evenings and weekends. Think of all those untold stories that such reporters feel no compulsion to go after. A number of these reporters are men and women of color who were wooed to help newspapers build up their diversity numbers. But there are many more white men in this category, too.

Among those who leave, and thus give up on telling their stories, are talented reporters like Jim Mitzelfeld, who covered state government for the *Detroit News*. As his story is recalled as part of a survey for the Project for Excellence in Journalism called "The State of the American Newspaper," by the early 1990s newspapers across the country, seeking ways of cutting costs, began cutting back on their coverage of statehouses, once a staple. Gannett, owner of the *Detroit News*, was no different. "They were having us crank out a daily story or two every day," Mitzelfeld said. "They wanted them short—six, eight inches, twelve if we were lucky—and then a lot of them didn't run." When he said he needed more space to tell both sides of a story, he said he was told "too bad." "There were times when they'd say, 'We don't have room for both sides; pick one side.' " Still, he managed to spend a couple of weeks following a tip about fraud in a legislative agency. The result was that five people went to prison and he won the 1994 Pulitzer Prize for beat reporting. But by then he had quit the news business. He became a lawyer.

The first line of resistance to the telling of certain stories is the editors, most of whom, until recently, were white men of similar age, background, and outlook. Even some of the first blacks to join the ranks of top editors, like some of the first women, have much more in common with the white guys than they do with the black and brown and female reporters who are trying to tell the untold stories. While I by no means knock efforts to bring the widest possible mix of men and women into the news business, it is important to keep in mind that color and gender diversity is not the same as diversity of ideas, diversity of perspective. I know black editors who know less about Harlem than many white folks do and could care less about how, or whether, it is covered.

The consequence of this is pernicious. The white bosses will argue that there can be no problem because there is a black editor in a key position and if he doesn't think what you've proposed is a story, then it's probably not a story. After all, he is black, too, isn't he? They don't realize that their favorite black editor, wanting to please the bosses and be just like them, is perhaps wary of pushing for too many black stories and doesn't want to be seen as an advocate for black reporters and editors. At the same time, the black reporters who have been arguing for having a black person in a key decision-making position feel that they have to watch the brother's back and not complain too much for fear of (1) appearing to be motivated by jealousy or (2) undermining him and convincing the white bosses that they really don't need a black person in a key position because the black staffers are still going to complain. Many stories never see the light of day because of such intraracial tension.

In September 1994, for example, the *Washington Post* ran an eight-part series by veteran reporter Leon Dash called "Rosa Lee's Story." It won the 1995 Pulitzer Prize for explanatory journalism. The series offered a harrowingly heartbreaking and disgusting portrait of one dysfunctional family, headed by Rosa Lee Cunningham. Dash was hailed for exposing this side of life. Many other black reporters were, to put it mildly, peeved. They said that Dash had fed into every stereotype held by his editors and, perhaps, a sizable portion of *Washington Post* readers. Dash argued that this was a story that needed to be told, and he went on telling such stories until he left the *Post* for academe. Many black reporters at the *Post* went on ignoring those stories, looking for something other than black pathology to write about. But if anyone wanted to do something similar to Dash's stories, editors might say, "We've done that story" and pass. Think of the stories they'd miss because of such an attitude.

Those stories could be like the one the *Times* and

every other New York news organization missed in January 1999 when Marvin Watson, a twenty-two-year-old black man, was killed in Crown Heights. In a situation such as this, when you have a black male homicide victim, editors, and too many reporters, assume they know the answers so they don't ask questions. Just another dead black man. Not news. But, because of guilt at the overwhelming media and political response to the death of a twenty-six-year-old white woman, Amy Watkins, in the same area, the *Times* decided to do a story that examined the difference in the responses to those tragic deaths. The result was, "One Precinct, Two Very Different Murder Cases," which appeared on page one.

In the end, we have a story that tells us that the death of Watson did not matter because he was black and poor and he didn't look "like a favorite friend or a relative in a picture on the mantel" of people who look like the dead woman. I think Amy Watkins would be appalled by that devaluation of another's life.

I don't know how that story came about, but I do know this: There was evidently no one around to question the reporters' premise or to guide them towards something beyond the obvious: she's white, he's black. The *Times* missed an opportunity to transcend race in showing that Watkins's death hit not just the white folks gentrifying her neighborhood, but the buppies and other residents, too. This didn't have to be a "white-woman-is-of-greater-value-than-a-black-man" piece. It could have shown the fears that all the young gentrifiers have, indeed that all city dwellers have, of the stranger attacking them on a darkened street. As for the Watson part of the story, rather than implying that crime is to be expected in the projects, I'd much rather have read about those families who are, in their own way, "gentrifying" the projects by trying their darnedest to live normal lives that revolve around family and friends and things like baby showers.

Now, when someone like me criticizes a story such as the one on the Watson-Watkins deaths, editors sometimes say, "That's the last time I assign a story that tries to put a human face on a black homicide. There's no satisfying those folks." So, for a while at least, those stories may go untold.

I really care about stories that convey life as it is being lived in an urban center such as New York City. As it is being lived today, not as it was once lived when the Irish controlled local politics, Jewish scholars thrived at City College, and the Bronx was the borough of parks. Those stories do not come most of the time. It is not unheard of for editors to say, when stories about people in certain parts of town are pitched, "Our readers don't care about. . . ." You can fill in the blanks: the South Bronx, hair braiding wars, tent revivals, cricket matches, fire-hydrant baptisms. They don't realize that readers are curious about the world beyond their living rooms and their doorsteps, and, if the story is well-told, readers will find it riveting, find that although it happens to have its locus in the South Bronx, it resonates in their own lives, whether they live in Syracuse or on Staten Island.

One reason editors react that way is that many of them don't have a clue about the lives of the people who are not part of their social world. They don't understand the leadership structure of other communities, which are defined not only by geography, but also by common interests. The Harwood Group, in a study conducted for the Pew Center for Civic Journalism, noted: "Many people think of 'leaders' as those who are elected officials, serve in official capacities within government institutions, or are heads of large companies and directors of community foundations. But those definitions represent perhaps the smallest segment of community leaders." Beyond these "official leaders" and even "civic leaders," who include leaders of religious institutions and neighborhood organizations, are two other categories often overlooked by the media. The Harwood Group labels them "connectors" and "catalysts." The former are "People who move in between organizations and civic conversations. They tend to be people who interact with multiple organizations, institutions and people—carrying and spreading ideas, messages and social norms from place to place." The latter, catalysts, are "Leaders whom people look to in their everyday lives for community expertise, historical perspective and wisdom. They often are responsible for encouraging others to get involved in civic life. Catalysts are the respected neighbors, co-workers and lay church leaders in people's lives."

It has been my experience that editors are wary of those folks who have no titles and no official positions and, thus, discourage reporters from relying upon them for stories that have not already been validated somewhere else. That tends to squelch enterprise and leaves reporters playing catch-up rather than producing cutting-edge stories. That is especially true regarding stories about people who don't look like editors or interact with them on a social basis.

Editors are also wary of stories in which the protagonists don't fit the profile that the editor, or sometimes the reporter, has in mind. Thus, for a Mother's Day story, at many papers you could not possibly feature Latino mothers being escorted out of church by their children or black mothers being treated to Sunday dinner at Sylvia's soul food restaurant, could you? For the opening of the public beach each spring, you couldn't possibly feature a photograph of someone who is not the palest white, could you?

Still, there is some good news. Editors, who often say they are guided by what marketing surveys indicate readers want, are good at telling you that something you feel passionate about is not news. But what is news these days? Who would have predicted that the president's puerile sexual activity would be the number one story in the nation for more than a year, right down to the cigars and the semen-stained dress? The definition of news is changing. While one might argue whether that is good or bad, reporters should take heart and muster the fortitude and creativity to take advantage of the flux. For sure, you will still be constrained by what editors like, as evidenced by what they consistently display on the front page and the feature pages. But the fuzziness over the definition of news gives you greater leeway to pitch the stories you want to tell. That's the optimistic way of looking at the situation. Call me Pollyanna.

4.
Washington Journalism

CHANGING IT IS HARDER THAN I THOUGHT

By James Warren

Washington, D.C., is a city where politicians believe in the to-get-along, go-along rule, and so it is probably not surprising that the attitude often spills over to Washington reporters. They can find plenty of other reasons for censoring their own work: the pressures of competition, desire for access to top politicians, and ambition to become a journalistic celebrity.

James Warren had never worked in Washington before the Chicago Tribune *sent him there to be its bureau chief. He had been the* Tribune*'s labor and legal affairs writer, then its national media writer, and then editor of its daily features section. Before that he was a reporter for the* Chicago Sun-Times *and the* Newark Star-Ledger. *What he has tried to do, Warren said, is apply the lessons he learned covering city halls and labor strikes to the often-clubby world of Washington reporting.*

When Howard Tyner, the *Chicago Tribune*'s editor in chief, asked me to try my hand in Washington, in 1994, there was no blueprint. There was just a desire to somehow turn out more stories that readers found interesting. His perception was that our product had become a bit too static, boring, a bit too beholden to daily agendas set by the likes of the *Washington Post* and *New York Times*. He's an honest fellow. Again, he didn't have any blueprint of his own.

The *Tribune* bureau at the time was a very traditional, newspaper-only bureau, doing pretty traditional stories, covering the same sort of obvious beats most everybody did and still does, namely, the White House, Congress, Pentagon, State Department. Like most of the others, it was heavy on politics and low on the sorts of agencies, like the Agriculture Department, that can actually impact our lives on a daily basis. To the extent I had any overarching desire in going to Washington, it was that our then sixteen-person contingent should inspect the town more as if we were foreign correspondents, reporting back to folks in the Midwest on an important place with a particular, even peculiar, culture and set of mores. It seemed, and seems, such a terribly easy notion to me. I would be woefully dishonest intellectually if I did not concede that it has been easier said than done.

For starters, I have tried to lead by example, both as a manager and as a reporter producing both a weekly column and, at times, like during the impeachment trial, writing daily, more impressionistic, off-the-news pieces. So there I am in the occasional weird mode of both editing a lot of our stories and writing a fair number of them. It makes for long days but, for one who can go stir-crazy being just a manager, stuck inside, it's therapeutic. More important, it keeps your hand in the game.

Very early on I met a certain resistance from within our bureau, from people who were very decent souls and very capable professionals but who had difficulty being quite as critical as I desired when it came to the key people on their beats. In addition, I generated, and still do, outright scorn among some in the journalism establishment. Early on I wrote about the fawning over White House staff members at Bill and Hillary Clinton's annual Christmas party, where journalists lined up dutifully for twenty or thirty minutes before they got to the head of the line and met the president and first lady, turned around, and had their glossy color photo snapped, the photo arriving at their homes about ten days later, most suitable for framing. After the photo, it was on to the huge tables of free food and booze and schmoozing with the folks many routinely covered. In what I am sure was a mere coincidence, and had nothing to do with the impeachment mess, the structure of the party was totally changed for Christmas of 1998. No line to meet the president and first lady. He quickly surfaced in an absurdly overcrowded tent, almost like at some overrun county fair, yelled out a few words, and was gone.

I also wrote about my first few bureau chief "backgrounders," sessions for supposedly A-list journalists, one of the first coming at the White House before that evening's State of the Union address, another in a private dining room at the Pentagon. At the first one, virtually all the president's men were there, it seemed, including the vice president, the chief spokesman, the national security adviser, and the chief of staff. They all played the classic Washington roles as unidentified "administration officials" to give us all the inside poop on the speech. This address, unlike all previous State of the Union speeches, they intoned earnestly, would not be a laundry list of promises to one and all. That was folderol. So was some of the deeply solicitous questioning of top aides on a first-name basis.

It was very clubby and a big reason why self-censorship can be one of journalism's biggest problems—the many subtle and not-so-subtle ways we may protect sources, protect people we want to stay friendly with. It may be all the more pernicious in Washington, where the stakes are indeed higher than they are at Chicago City Hall or the county building in Los Angeles, since big, national issues are being deliberated and huge decisions impacting all our lives and costing billions are being made. All the more pernicious in a place where so many reporters are smitten by having access to key decision-makers, by getting the little scoop that can win them praise among their bosses, even make a career. All the more pernicious in a place where the newsmakers can play the game pretty tough and may be inclined to simply shut you out, no longer give you much access, if you do something they do not like. All the more pernicious in a place where, because the stakes are so high, an individual media organization may get nervous if the top decision-makers are shutting out their guy and, in the process, making them look bad when competitors get certain stories.

It's not an easy matter to deal with in an unequivocal fashion, unless one simply decides to refuse to deal with people, refuse to ever go on background or off the record. Just take the Washington fracas involving two friends, one a British journalist named Christopher Hitchens, the other a White House aide named Sidney Blumenthal, over Blumenthal's allegedly telling his old chum over lunch that Monica Lewinsky was a stalker. Then Hitchens went public about the conversation. You can raise questions about Hitchens's selling out his old friend, but what about the many Washington journalists, especially folks at the White House, who also knew that some of the president's aides were badmouthing Lewinsky but won't 'fess up now since they are wary of rupturing relations with sources? I assure you, there are probably more than a few.

Anyway, to get back to that State of the Union briefing: I did write about it and haven't been invited back since.

Then there was my morning at the Pentagon, where the secretary of defense and head of the Joint Chiefs wanted to extol the virtues of NATO-related actions the president would take in Europe a few days hence. Since the hot topic that week was nuclear skullduggery by the North Koreans, questions quickly flew as to what our government really knew about what was going on in Korea. First, we went "on background," then on "deep background." At meeting's end, I asked a *Washington Post* editorial writer who'd been there how exactly he would attribute the little tidbit or two that came out on deep background. The term, perhaps a definition of rhetorical self-imprisonment, is one foreign to the daily labors of those covering City Hall or the county building in municipalities nationwide.

The *Post* person paused, fumbled for a bit, then with a straight face declared, "Oh, you say something like, 'It's known that.' " He paused, smiled, realized the semantical silliness of the game he had once again agreed to play, and said, almost ruefully, "You're right. This is another reason they should rotate reporters out of here every few years." I wrote about that session and haven't been invited back there either.

If I went on some crusade against these briefings, would it have any impact? I am convinced it would not. You'd have to get everybody to agree not to take part in such gatherings and that will never happen. Since they are always of *some* utility, some organization will always claim they serve the interests of their organization. As long as one organization is willing to go, that will justify the others going for competitive reasons.

But if the coziness between subject and reporter, as well as journalists' willingness to gain and protect their prized access—often, I think, access to get lied to—at virtually any price, are generally not appreciated outside the Beltway (by the way, how many Americans have a clue what the Beltway even is?), the wheel of fortune that an influential cadre of reporters zealously gets to spin is even less well known.

So, when I stumbled upon the following and, wet behind the ears, passed the news on to *Tribune* readers, I quickly was threatened with caricature as some self-promoting, inexperienced iconoclast:

- Lesley Stahl of CBS's *60 Minutes* took twenty thousand dollars from Cigna, the insurance giant, for moderating an in-house video conference in which six purported experts, all opponents of that year's Clinton health-care plan, bashed it as they "debated" it. Even Stahl was moved to the embarrassing admission to the audience at the end of the ninety-minute Clinton thrashing that it was too bad that nobody from the administration had taken part. But she knew that she, and she assumed the viewers, had certainly learned a lot. I wondered how in the world a reporter could be taking money from a company so deeply entwined in the biggest story of the day, health care, which her esteemed network was covering.

- Cokie Roberts of ABC and National Public Radio, who in Washington is as close to social-media aristocracy as one gets (daughter of both a famous congressman and a well-liked congresswoman) and also queen of the moonlighters, took twenty thousand dollars from one health-care association right smack in the middle of the very health-care debate she was covering as the network's congressional reporter. In the fall of 1994, she and her husband, Steven V. Roberts, a reporter for *U.S. News and World Report,* took forty-five thousand dollars from a Chicago bank ("honoraria, 'til death do us part," I guess) for essentially serving as its marketing arm, offering wisdom on the current state of Washington politics to prospective bank clients in Chicago. Chicago is obviously a favorite and she was back there again several months later, this time at a women's job conference subsidized by about fifteen area businesses, including, yes, the *Chicago Tribune.* So much for the influence I have in-house.

  Not too many months later, the Robertses' treasury was enriched by, of all firms, Philip Morris, at the very time that company was suing ABC for ten billion dollars as a result of a newsmagazine story accusing the tobacco industry of intentionally spiking the nicotine content of cigarettes. The Robertses were the scheduled paid speakers at a private gathering for Philip Morris customers in West Palm Beach, Florida. After I was slipped an internal brochure on the gathering and brought it to ABC's attention, Cokie Roberts said that this had to be a mistake, that she knew nothing about the engagement, and it had been her husband who attended and took the company's money. When I informed the previously silent company that she had essentially accused them of misrepresenting her appearance, officials informed me that they had booked the two of them and that Cokie had personally called in the day before, saying she was sick and could not make it. Her health apparently returned soon and she was back on the circuit, generally collecting thirty-five thousand dollars a pop.

- Tim Russert, genial host of NBC's vastly improved *Meet the Press,* which he's turned into arguably the best Sunday show, took more than twenty thousand dollars from the American Bankers Association for moderating a mock *Meet the Press* at the group's annual meeting. His guests during the twenty-minute session were Robert Dole, then Senate majority leader, and Treasury Secretary Robert Rubin, who then held another administration position. Both Dole and Rubin were barred by federal ethics rules from taking a penny from

> such a group for such an appearance. "But I didn't ask questions any differently than I would on the show," Russert protested when I confronted him.

This, of course, is not quite the point. But I guess some deem it uninformed to suggest that a reporter simply not be involved in any business transaction with anyone he or she covers, any group whose interests the reporter covers, or anybody with a clear stake in congressional legislation.

At the *Tribune,* our rules even forbid us from fundraising for charities or sitting on community boards. Admittedly, we don't (and shouldn't, I suspect) go quite as far as the editor of the *Washington Post,* who does not vote, lest he show preference for somebody his paper reports on. But the editor, Leonard Downie, would probably be tagged a well-intentioned, self-righteous prig by the lecture-circuit army, which includes CNN's *Capital Gang* and *The McLaughlin Group,* which both have active road shows. *The McLaughlin Group* group can usually be had for twenty thousand dollars for forty minutes of middlebrow mud wrestling and has taken from an impressive array of special interests, including the American Association of Retired Persons and the National Pest Control Association. As for Downie, a decent and bright fellow, he coincidentally finds himself taking this high road on not voting while letting his media writer, a good reporter named

Howard Kurtz, take money from CNN for hosting a weekly show there. One more time: the media writer takes a substantial sum from a major company he covers. I have debated this in print with Downie and find his response bordering on sophistry and, at minimum, a classic example of situational ethics.

Deciding to pare, if not eliminate, this sort of stuff takes more than good intentions. It also takes some backbone, something that may be in decreasing quantities as financial and competitive pressures squeeze all media. I think the *Washington Post* example may be a decent case study. Hey, who cares about right and wrong when you've got a dwindling market share, circulation, and ratings? Leave that stuff for pontificating journalism professors. What is surely the inevitable mix of traditional editorial and business-marketing considerations can mean that getting out the brand name, be it in front of a Rotary luncheon or paltry CNBC audience, is increasingly valued. Editors will look the other way as long as their guy is on the air or getting their name out.

As a bureau chief, I'd have my head in the sand if I thought my one and only role is to try to assign and edit great stories. I must be conscious of spreading the good word about a terrific product with which I'm associated, especially in a world in which kids would rather stare at today's dysfunctional circus on *Oprah, Geraldo,* or the *Jenny Jones Show* than strain their mental capacities by attempting to read newspapers. For this reason, I have rationalized going on

TV myself. Also, the *Chicago Tribune* has at the same time become a different sort of bureau, Washington's first joint print-television bureau. We have combined with Tribune Broadcasting, which has exploded in size, now consisting of nineteen major stations, fourteen of which do news every day, including huge stations in New York, Chicago, Los Angeles, Denver, Boston, Philadelphia, New Orleans, and Sacramento. In addition, out of our bureau, we syndicate two shows, one a health show, the other a business show.

I refuse to take a penny for speeches, even though the TV exposure I have received has brought a fair number of invitations and chances to make significant sums. For sure, Washington offers that lure for some journalists, especially those with regular TV exposure. And it can be head-turning. But I do think that the interests of our paper—which, remember, is not really read that much inside Washington—and my own personal interests, such as getting people to return phone calls, can be served by getting my mug on television, even if I personally spurn the wheel of fortune that can easily bring five thousand dollars a speech even for a modestly known person like me. The question, to me at least, then becomes whether one prostitutes oneself by being intellectually dishonest, namely b.s.'ing on topics one really doesn't know much about.

That can be an occupational hazard on TV, especially if you don't do your homework. One of my bigger challenges has come of late, with invitations to appear on the MSNBC version of McLaughlin's show, a slightly different show than his normal week-end one, which has been running Monday through Thursday. For starters, some friends were asking how I could appear on that food fight of a show I had pil-loried? They had a certain point. For me, the impor-tant thing was seeing if I could avoid the premeditated combative silliness of it all by being prepared and at least trying to be thoughtful. I'd like to think I've accomplished that, but I don't doubt that some will cry "Hypocrisy!"

When I went to Washington, I wanted to change our beat structure all around. I wanted to have beats on subjects like the family, money, and technopolis. The family beat would take everything that happened in Washington, or didn't happen, and relate it to the real lives of real families. Money would be an intense focus on how the political system is driven by money, how it corrodes the process, how it wins votes, how it buys congressmen and senators. Technopolis would be all about the growth of technology and, using Washington as a base, the reporter would go out in the country and see the impact of technology on our lives, with special sensitivity to issues such as the growing challenges to personal privacy. At the same time I would urge my bosses to use the existing wire services, such as the Associated Press and *The New York Times* services, both of which we pay hefty sums to get, for many of the very orchestrated news stories each day, be they a congressional hearing, press conference, the unveiling of some report, whatever. That would be a way to free up our people for what I consider real enterprise.

Five years later, I would give myself a grade of B. I did create what amounted to a family beat, but that person left the business and I have been unable, for budgetary reasons, to replace her. The technopolis beat is essentially there, with a special accent on privacy, but the stories are difficult to get in the paper sometimes because a more traditional mindset back in Chicago often prefers a story with an obvious news angle, and many of these stories are softer, are about trends, and don't have that angle. The money beat didn't work out for staffing reasons. More important, we still do too many things because everybody else does them. We obviously are not alone.

If you look at the big paper in town, the *Washington Post,* and look at how it distributes its resources, you see another problem. Twenty years ago, it would surely have covered pretty closely each cabinet agency, not just the Defense and State Departments, but the Environmental Protection Agency and the Agriculture Department and the Energy Department, among others. Now the *Post* doesn't even do the Ag Department on a regular basis. Same thing with Energy and the EPA. Somehow we got away from all that, in part, I suspect, because of an ironic impulse to do more of what we thought readers wanted and in part due to the pressures brought by television. We had to become more personalized, we thought, and more thematic. The supposedly daily, incremental stories went out of fashion—exactly the sort of stories that can, over time, help a reporter cultivate sources and generate other, bigger stories.

At the same time, there seems to be more and more coverage of politics, and personalities, than ever before, and less about actual legislation and governing and the substance of things. We are more into the political infighting and declaring who wins and loses and making sure to profile them. It's a type of reporting that seems to inspire a new sort of reporter, one more attuned to and reflective of the whole celebritization of journalism, a reporter more given to doing speculative stories on whether this or that public figure will run for office rather than something substantive.

We are more likely to give big awards to the writer of the big, sassy feature story on Senator Such and Such, rather than to the fellow who has been cranking out little, accurate, responsible, daily stories on the evolution of a big piece of legislation, such as a change in the telecommunications law. Those reporters who have the most cachet and influence seem, more and more, to be the ones with the big personalities who are on TV. Again, I say this a bit defensively since I get my mug on TV quite a bit, but I also pride myself on doing a good amount of actual reporting, sitting in courtrooms for hours, plowing through governmental records, checking out boxes of old stuff at the National Archives.

A fair number of people in the business don't do much reporting and are very much sound-bite, TV creatures. It is sad that they, not the great reporters covering courthouses or county boards or doing local investigations at smaller papers, are somehow the journalism stars of the era, the ones who get the requests to make speeches, the ones, even more sadly, who get asked to speak at college graduations. In my day, it was theologians and poets and authors and priests. Now, the favorite category is TV anchor. Yikes.

If I could do anything I wanted in Washington, I would cover more of the regulatory agencies and see how they do and do not impact our lives. Maybe I would conclude that some of them are rat holes, holding pens for thousands of inept bureaucrats. Maybe I would find out something different. But this visceral rage so many Americans have about their government deserves some empirical, true-blue reporting. What do these agencies do? I would also send more of my reporters, regardless of their beats, out into the country regularly to see what the connection is between their beats and real Americans. This is an expensive proposition, and not every paper or news organization can do it. But I think those that can should. The folks who cover Capitol Hill tend only to head off around election time, to cover supposedly interesting races. I would have them leave regularly to see what people are thinking, whether that jibes with what the congressmen and senators are saying and, more important, what the impact of actual legislation is on citizens' lives.

If there is one ultimate bit of chagrin I have with everything in Washington, it involves how many damn smart people there are covering the town. Many more smart people than before. Probably much more ethical than before. Despite all the hoopla over various ethical mishaps lately, it wasn't too long ago—back in the 1970s—when reporters for Detroit newspapers routinely called the publicity departments of the major carmakers to get freebies to use on their vacations. That's just one example of how slimy things have been.

But for all the talents of Washington reporters, their endeavors seem, especially at the mainstream newspaper, magazine, and TV outlets, to be concentrated in such a narrow area, 80 percent of those reporters covering maybe 15 percent of the news. So lots of things routinely don't get covered, because they don't seem sexy, or they might not make page one or Dan Rather's newscast, or they are too hard. How many mainstream organizations did the painstaking legwork to get to the bottom of what the hell we did with that weird bombing of the pharmaceutical factory in the Sudan in August 1998, and then the bombings, right during the finale of the House impeachment debate and vote, of Iraq? It was easier to focus on impeachment. It was right there, it was simple, it was in front of you, it was like going to a Broadway play. And it didn't involve raising the question of whether the White House had committed some big whoppers in dealing with the American public. That would have involved real digging.

Now, digging for the truth is nothing very new or cutting edge. In fact, it's pretty old-fashioned. For those who really and truly want to be successes in this business, I don't think you could do anything better than to get yourself in a position, even if it's at a weekly paper or radio station or TV station in the middle of nowhere, where you will have to work your butt off, doing tons of stories, learning your craft, talking to enough politicians so you wind up with a pretty good bullshit detector so you know when they're lying, learning your way around the records room in a courthouse, or waiting in some cold hotel lobby until three in the morning so you can get one of the negotiators in a big labor dispute to tell you what's going on. It's very old-fashioned. And it does get done in Washington—just not quite as much as it should.

5.

Black and White and Red All Over

The Ongoing Struggle to Integrate America's Newsrooms

By Vanessa Williams

Although Vanessa Williams knew she liked to write when she was growing up in St. Petersburg, Florida, she never gave any thought to a career in journalism, because, she said, she did not know African-Americans could be journalists. Certainly she had not seen any African-Americans in journalism. A program run by her hometown paper, the St. Petersburg Times, *got her started. She has since balanced government reporting at places like the* Philadelphia Inquirer *and the* Washington Post, *where she covers urban affairs and politics, with participation in programs to encourage other minorities to enter journalism.*

As president of the National Association of Black Journalists from 1997 to 1999, she worked to provide members with the skills and confidence to become newsroom leaders. She also kept pressuring newspapers and broadcast stations to hire more minorities, arguing that without newsroom diversity, journalists were doing their jobs wearing racial blinders.

One day last year I got a call from the media reporter for the *New York Times* asking me to comment on an idea by the publisher of the *Los Angeles Times*. The publisher had suggested setting goals, with financial incentives, in an effort to urge reporters and editors to quote more people of color in their stories. The media reporter told me that some journalists were outraged at the suggestion. They argued that reporters should seek out people who have knowledge of the subject as opposed to choosing spokespersons based on the color of their skin.

Of course it wouldn't make sense to interview an African-American grade school teacher for a story on the newest techniques in brain surgery. But what's the harm in working a little harder to find a black neurosurgeon? And for all the stories newspapers do on education, why don't we see more grade school teachers who are black quoted on the subject? Most troubling in all of this is why was it necessary to even propose, let alone be called upon to defend, such an initiative to journalists at the *L.A. Times*, which serves a city in which the majority of residents are people of color?

As I considered this latest uproar, I thought to myself, "Here we go again. Another skirmish in the long-running diversity war."

Many African-American journalists are familiar with the stories of black journalists who entered the profession as shock troops during the late 1960s and early 1970s. It was a period of social and racial unrest in our nation and major cities across the country were ablaze with street riots. Mainstream news organizations found themselves ill-equipped to cover the story and frantically recruited black men and women to go into the smoldering inner cities to document the frustration, fear, and rage of Black America.

Once inside these newsrooms, black journalists started to ask some questions about the larger issues of the news media's commitment and how good a job they were doing in covering communities of color. The frustrations of both the journalists and their communities was backed up by the 1968 report of the National Advisory Commission on Civil Disorders, commonly called the Kerner Commission, which chastised the news media for being "shockingly backward" in hiring and promoting black journalists and in covering the black community. So began the modern newsroom diversity movement.

During the last three decades, newspapers have made strides in employing more black journalists as reporters, photographers, and editors. Coverage has improved since the days when stories about African-Americans were relegated to back pages or designated "black" pages of daily newspapers. Still, the presence and influence of African-Americans in the newsroom and the news pages remain nagging issues for daily newspapers. We see it in the high level of mistrust and anger—and the resulting low circulation—in some black communities toward their local newspapers. We see it in newsroom surveys, which show a high level of frustration among black journalists, many of whom feel they have little value to, or influence in, their news organizations.

Black and white and red all over: the continuing struggle to integrate America's newsrooms. It's a play on an old riddle. In this case, the black and white refers to race, although I might add that in recent years the industry, faced with the rapidly changing demographics of the country, must also be concerned with Asians, Hispanics, and Native Americans. The red refers to the heated emotions that color this struggle: frustration, embarrassment, anger.

What does this have to do with the news product? Everything. News organizations' continued inability to integrate African-Americans and other journalists of color into their newsrooms and to more accurately and fairly represent racial and ethnic communities threatens the credibility and viability of daily, general-circulation newspapers. How can a newspaper claim to be a journal of record for a given city or region if it routinely ignores or misrepresents large segments of the population in the geographic area it covers? How do newspapers expect to survive economically if they fail to capture the growing racial and ethnic communities that, according to demographic projections, will constitute a majority of the country's population by the middle of the next century?

Our greatest concern about the industry's failure to grasp the gravity of its diversity deficit should be the potential harm to society. Many Americans continue to operate out of misinformation and misunderstanding when it comes to perceptions and relationships between racial groups, between religious groups, between men and women, straight and gay people, young and old people, middle-class and working-class people. The press, by failing to provide more accurate, thorough, and balanced coverage of our increasingly diverse communities, has abdicated its responsibility to foster an exchange of information and perspectives that is so necessary in a democracy.

Despite the presence of more journalists of color and more women in the newsroom during the last thirty years, most newspapers continue to interpret the world through the eyes of middle- and upper-middle-class white people, mostly men, who hold the vast majority of management positions. That means the "who," "what," "why," "when," "where," and "how" must grab their attention some way to be considered news. There are simply not enough journalists of color in positions of power to effect significant, major, radical change in coverage. The most recent census by the American Society of Newspaper Editors showed that journalists of color represent only 9 percent of newsroom supervisors. Indeed, the survey reported, 40 percent of the nation's newsrooms employ no journalists of color.

I do not mean to suggest that these managers willfully or consciously make decisions to exclude or limit coverage of communities of color. Rather, they decide what to put on the front page based on what they think is important, interesting, unusual, or amusing. Reporters often joke that news is defined by what editors notice on their way to work. If the editor arrives at the office rattled from having driven over pothole-riddled roads, then bad roads become big news. If, however, editors don't drive past the bustling business district of a Hispanic, Asian, or African-American community, they might not see what city services are lacking, or are working well, in those communities.

A friend of mine, a black woman who has worked as a local news editor at three urban dailies, recalled being frustrated at one Northeastern daily's coverage of a municipal transit strike. Most of the stories focused on the plight of stranded suburban commuters, with little regard for how low-income folks in the city were getting around. She dispatched a reporter to a working-class black community and found that one man had borrowed his son's new bike to get to his job. Another reporter ended up walking with a woman for thirty blocks as she hustled to her job as a maid at a downtown hotel.

Most editors will bristle at the suggestion that they are insensitive to the interests of people in communities of color and argue that the media's treatment of African-Americans and other racial and ethnic groups has improved dramatically. That is true. Newspapers no longer use the word "nigger" to describe black people. Newspapers have discontinued the practice of segregating a page or two for "News of the Negro Community." Most newspapers today will run the obligatory Kwanzaa stories in December and Black History Month stories in February. So, people say, what do you want?

Neither black journalists nor black media consumers are impressed. Increasingly, neither are journalists and readers who represent other communities of color.

What about stories, language, or images that on the surface appear to have nothing to do with race, but still offend African-Americans? What about practices we routinely use to determine what is news, and devices we often rely on to tell stories that outrage black readers? For example, a 1997 study by a Yale professor named Martin Gilens found that African-Americans were disproportionately represented in photographs depicting poverty and welfare dependence. Gilens's research showed that African-Americans account for 65 percent of poor Americans shown on network television news and 62 percent of people depicted in newsmagazines. In reality, he reported, African-Americans make up only 29 percent of the nation's poor. Gilens asserts that such stereotyping influences perceptions about public policies, such as welfare.

The news media rely heavily on African-Americans and other people of color to explore the range of social pathologies, such as criminal behavior, illegal drug activity, and teenage pregnancy. Reporters seek to take readers inside the lives of the people gripped by these circumstances, spending days, weeks, or months hanging out with a teenage drug dealer, watching the decline of a drug addict, shadowing the struggling single mother. Many of these stories are compelling and sensitively told; often they are told by African-American journalists.

As a journalist I firmly believe that we must seek the truth about these issues, so I am not arguing that we should not present a realistic picture of the dire conditions in many poor African-American neighborhoods, no matter how ugly that picture may be. I also know that reporters and editors believe that these stories will help spur communities and officials to take action to address these problems. What I take issue with is that these types of stories, particularly in large urban dailies, are seldom done about white people. It's not that I relish the idea of white people looking beaten down on the front page, but I wonder if people in positions of influence would be so complacent if they saw that these social sicknesses could affect *their* children, parents, siblings, and friends.

We do not present an accurate portrait of these social problems by presenting them only with black faces. We mislead the public into thinking that drug addiction, teen pregnancy, violent crime, and myriad other pathologies only happen to "those people." Why do the media continue to get the story wrong? Why do the media continue to infuriate and alienate residents in communities of color, many of whom are convinced that the "white media" actively try to besmirch the image of people of color in America?

Some of my colleagues argue that the news media's coverage of these issues is geared to reassure white Americans that everything's OK with them. My colleagues feel that we've turned the oath to afflict the comfortable and comfort the afflicted on its head and that we too often afflict the afflicted and comfort the comfortable. We say to them, "It's not your fault, it's not your problem, it only happens to these kinds of people and they bring it upon themselves."

I don't think the vast majority of journalists purposely set out to make people of color look bad. Indeed, most reject the notion that they are racially insensitive. Instead, I think the vast majority of journalists are white and middle-class and that they bring their experiences and prejudices to newsrooms where there are few, if any, checks and balances in the form of journalists who come from different racial and class groups.

I've heard some white journalists challenge the newsroom diversity discussion as being too narrowly focused on race and ethnicity. They argue that because most journalists of color are college educated and make middle-class salaries, their viewpoints are not necessarily that different from white college-educated professionals who make middle-class salaries. That ignores the fact that this society continues to be segregated largely along racial lines. Even in the workplace, there is little cross-cultural interaction: How often do colleagues of different racial groups go out to lunch or out for drinks after work? How many visit each other's homes on weekends? How many live in the same neighborhoods, send their children to the same schools, worship at the same churches? Polls suggest that most black and white people, even within the same social class, have sharply divergent perceptions on such issues as discrimination, police relations, affirmative action, crime, welfare, and politics. So you do need people of color in a newsroom. And you also need intellectual diversity, and people need to feel free to be who they are and bring what they know to the story, to the newsroom.

I firmly believe that newsrooms should contain journalists of different ages, classes, gender, sexual orientation, and religions. Without a diverse newsroom, where journalists can discuss and challenge each other's assumptions, reporting, and interpretation of the facts, newspapers will not be able to provide more accurate, balanced, and thorough coverage of their communities. That means news organizations are effectively silencing significant segments of the populations in their circulation areas and are depriving white readers of accurate, balanced, and thorough information about their neighbors.

Another area in which communities of color often feel slighted is in the coverage of crime, particularly victims of crime. One of the most common complaints is that newspapers give more prominence to the murders of white middle-class residents than they do to victims of another race or ethnic group. The slayings of white suburban mothers, young urban professionals, and blond-haired children command front-page spreads and follow-up stories, including in-depth profiles and interviews with friends and neighbors, and mournful accounts of their funerals. Meanwhile the violent deaths of inner-city residents are written in the sterile format of crime briefs, if they are covered at all. During the year that the national news media focused on the mysterious death of Jon-Benet Ramsey, black activists and residents in Chicago decried the lack of attention for a nine-year-old black girl who was raped, beaten, and left for dead in a stairwell at the Cabrini-Green public housing development. In Washington, D.C., a white middle-class teenager crashed his car and killed some of his classmates who were riding with him, generating days of stories about the students and the dangers of careless driving. Meanwhile residents of a poor inner-city neighborhood lambasted both the Washington, D.C., police department and the *Post* for paying little attention to the killing of several young black women.

Why the disparity? Because the people who make decisions about what is newsworthy more readily identify with victims who look like them and live like them and are utterly frightened or outraged when bad things happen to them. The coverage reflects that fear and outrage. The headlines scream: "How is this possible? She's the same age as my daughter! He could be my son! This is not supposed to happen to people like us!"

The same is true of how the mainstream news media responds to whites who commit violent, public crimes. Remember the spate of shootings last year by white schoolboys in the South and Midwest? The response was shock and concern. News stories sought to try to explain what made these presumably good children go bad. We saw this trend again in the 1999 coverage of the shootings at Columbine High School in Littleton, Colorado. The media gingerly described the two shooters as boys who hung out with a "clique," as opposed to a "gang." They were not street-hardened youths, they were "alienated teenagers" or "boys." This did not escape some African-American readers and viewers who quietly grumbled, "If they had been black. . . ."

Such sensitive treatment of people of color who are victims or perpetrators is reserved for those who, in the eyes of the news media, did not deserve their fate. They in some way defy the stereotypes, they are a credit to their communities, or they exhibit qualities like those of white middle-class people. "He was a straight-A student. . . . She worked two jobs and went to school at night. . . . He opened his home to troubled youth." Otherwise, newsroom decision-makers seem to readily accept the fact that violence is as normal to "those people" as the changing of the seasons. The media cover the epidemic incidence of deaths of U.S. citizens, people who live just a few miles or a few minutes across town, with less urgency and more detachment than we do wars, riots, and other atrocities in countries thousands of miles away.

These are more dramatic examples of how the news media's lack of diversity skews the perceptions of people in a community about themselves and about other members of the community. Subtle slights and mistakes also occur with frequency, driving a wedge between newspapers and some segments of their community.

A few years ago a friend of mine assumed the editorship of a newspaper in southern New Jersey and found herself in the middle of a struggle to win the trust of Hispanic residents. Although Hispanics make up a large percentage of the town, the paper had no Spanish-speaking reporters on staff. Hispanic residents were constantly complaining that their names were misspelled, that reporters misquoted them or quoted them out of context, and that the newspaper did not write about the little things, like weddings or graduations, or the big things, such as the lack of Spanish-language voting instructions for municipal elections, that were important to their community. "There was just this general feeling that we would not do well by them, that we would not be fair, that we did not understand enough about them," she told me.

In one instance, the Hispanic community accused the paper of siding with town officials, who wanted to curtail an annual Hispanic festival. My friend took the extraordinary step of printing the transcript of a meeting between city officials and festival organizers on the issue. Her efforts bought limited good will, but she laments not having been able to recruit a Spanish-speaking reporter before she left the paper after three years.

This type of standoff is going on in communities all over the country where Hispanic and Asian populations have exploded over the past two decades and are projected to grow even faster during the next two decades. By the middle of the next century the percentage of people of color is projected to surpass that of white, native-born Americans. Newspapers are woefully lagging in their efforts to assemble newsroom staffs that have knowledge of and have credibility with these communities, which already constitute majorities in many cities in the West and Southwest United States. Needless to say, the relationship between black communities and newspapers, despite three decades of efforts to increase the number of black journalists and improve coverage, continues to be either tenuous or contemptuous.

For an industry that is rapidly losing readers, general-circulation newspapers are only hastening their own demise. In some cities, like San Francisco, ethnic newspapers with large circulations fill the gulf that general-circulation newspapers have left between themselves and immigrant communities.

Hiring more journalists of color and putting them

in decision-making positions is crucial to improving coverage of communities of color. But it is only a first step. Newsroom managers also must foster and encourage intellectual diversity that takes advantage of the skills, knowledge, and experiences that journalists of color bring to the job. Recent surveys of journalists of color show little change in attitudes since a groundbreaking survey in 1985 by the Maynard Institute for Journalism Education. Then as now, journalists of color reported a high level of frustration. They feel that their insights are not sought out or respected, that their judgments are questioned, and that the kinds of stories they want to pursue are not valued by the news organization.

Let me give you an example of how different insights affect news coverage. A couple of years ago, Marion Barry, then the Washington, D.C., mayor and a staunch liberal, announced his support for a proposal by a Republican member of the city council to institute the death penalty for persons convicted of shooting law enforcement officers. My editors saw this as an attempt by Barry to curry favor with white voters. I argued that there was little Barry could do, short of resigning, to win the favor of white voters. The more interesting question to me was why he thought he could advocate using capital punishment, with its attendant racial history, and not jeopardize his standing with black voters, his most loyal base of support. I won the coin toss and proceeded to report the story. What I found was that growing frustration and fear about crime in black communities had resulted in more African-Americans stating their support of capital punishment.

I further urged the newspaper to include a question about capital punishment in a citywide poll that was being planned about the same time Barry made his pronouncement. The paper found that more city residents said they favored capital punishment than in previous years. The results spawned a separate news story on that issue.

On the surface this doesn't seem like a remarkable or noteworthy victory. This is how journalism is supposed to work, editors and reporters testing their intuitions, discussing and dissecting the facts, working together to produce the best story. But it doesn't always go that smoothly or easily. Editors are sometimes too busy, too skeptical, too impatient, or too certain of their own vision of a story to engage in the kind of give-and-take that could lead to more textured and sophisticated stories about communities of color. Most journalists, despite their straightforward, even aggressive, behavior in pursuing a story, are reluctant to pick fights with their editors. The qualities that make us good reporters in the corridors of city hall or out on the streets are not necessarily welcomed in the newsroom. You can be labeled a troublemaker, not a team player, and be accused of being too sensitive or too black. Certainly not all, but many, journalists of color are particularly concerned about rocking the boat. They want to be trusted and respected in the newsroom, not dismissed as rabble-rousers or complainers.

When our instincts and experiences are respected, however, it can make a difference in how news organizations approach race-related stories. A striking example of how journalists of color across the country influenced mainstream perceptions of a news event was the October 1995 Million Man March, led by Louis Farrakhan, the controversial Nation of Islam leader.

When Farrakhan announced his plans to bring one million African-American men to Washington for a major demonstration, he was met with skepticism and, in some cases, derision. Farrakhan, who has been described as anti-Semitic and who is often depicted as a fringe figure in the black nationalist movement, was not taken seriously by news executives. Initial reports cast doubt on his ability to marshal such a demonstration, suggesting that African-Americans would not heed his call. Some raised questions about his motives for the march, which Farrakhan said was being staged to provide black men an opportunity to rededicate themselves to their families and their communities. Yet black men embraced the notion and in communities around the country there was excitement and a sense of mission as men prepared to participate in the event. It was primarily black men at newspapers around the country, often young black men, who told editors that, notwithstanding mainstream views of Farrakhan, the idea of the march had touched a nerve in African-American men.

A black male colleague at the *Washington Post* told me that it took some lobbying of editors before they saw that, apart from Farrakhan, the possibility of the march itself had become a big story in the African-American community. He credits the metropolitan editor at the time, an African-American, for fighting the battle at the top, while he and another black male reporter kept insisting to their editors that the event had sparked excitement in the community.

"We were talking to our editors about how there indeed was something going on, how on the streets we were seeing posters, how people were talking about it in the community, on black radio," he said. "If I and other black reporters weren't here, they probably would not have known about it as early . . . and they would have had no framework to analyze it. They would not be able to understand what they were hearing."

In advance of the march, stories were written about men raising money to rent buses, making plans to take their sons and boys from their neighborhood, having discussions about the responsibilities of manhood. Though Farrakhan, federal officials, and the news media would disagree on the exact number of men who participated in the march, pictures on television and in newspapers unmistakably showed that far more men had heeded the call than was originally expected. The Million Man

March became a national story, but the real story took place on the local level in the months preceding the event, when grassroots activists, everyday working fathers, and typical teenage boys suddenly caught the attention of the news media. They were there all along, but they typically don't make news unless one of them runs afoul of the law or does an extraordinary good deed that commands the media's attention.

It is often said among journalists of color—sometimes in jest, often in frustration—that we have to be twice as good as our white counterparts. In a sense, that's true. Journalists of color must demonstrate knowledge of mainstream history, current events, and culture to be considered qualified to work in the newsroom. We also are expected to be able to explain or translate events and issues in communities of color. But, with people of color expected to be the majority by the middle of the twenty-first century, it would seem that a "qualified" journalist would possess knowledge about the history and culture of African-American, Latino, Asian, and Native-American people. At the least, good journalists would understand why it is important to begin building sources within those communities now, as opposed to waiting until it's too late.

I think too many news editors and reporters look at diversity as something that has to be done to satisfy belligerent interest groups rather than an opportunity to educate their communities and engage new readers. If we don't change our attitudes and practices, newspapers will find it difficult to maintain credibility and relevance in rapidly changing communities and, as a result, newspapers will find it difficult to survive. Diversity is not about being politically correct or caving in to special interest groups. It is about newspapers being just plain correct in reflecting the diversity of their communities and acting to protect their own interests. Otherwise, we will be the ones stuck in a gilded ghetto, cut off from and ignored by a new multicultural country.

6.

Journalism Lite

How the Old Rules Were Thrown Out and the Press Lost Public Trust

By Sydney H. Schanberg

In the four decades Sydney H. Schanberg has been in journalism, he has, he said, seen an unhappy retreat from the old standards, standards that respected privacy, avoided anonymous sources, and took responsibility for the truth of what was printed or aired. No citing the public's right to know for irrelevant inquiries into the sex lives of public figures. No quoting stories that haven't been verified.

But, unlike many in the profession, Schanberg turns the arrow of blame for shoddy work toward journalists themselves. Their failure to take individual stands and their failure to report critically on the press's performance have, he argued, created a climate in which shoddy journalistic performance can be excused, even rewarded.

Schanberg began his career as a copyboy for the New York Times, *in 1959, and he spent his next twenty-six years at the paper. As a reporter, he covered local, national, and international issues. While on the foreign staff in 1974, he was one of a handful of Western journalists to witness the collapse of Cambodia, and, against the orders of his editors, he refused to leave. He was detained for two weeks by the Khmer Rouge; his reporting when he left won him the Pulitzer Prize for international reporting. Later he returned to the area to find Dith Pran, his friend and a* Times *photographer, who had been captured. His account of that journey became the book,* The Life and Death of Dith Pran, *and then the movie,* The Killing Fields.

Schanberg became metropolitan editor of the Times *and then, in 1981, a* Times *columnist. In 1986, after the* Times *objected to some columns he wrote about real-estate development, he left the paper. He moved to* New York Newsday, *where he also wrote a column. After that he worked on books and other special projects before becoming investigations editor for APBNews Online, devoted to crime and justice issues.*

Whenever I am asked about what reporters do for a living, and why anyone would pay them for such work, I usually respond by telling the following story, which was related to me in the *New York Times* newsroom when I was a copyboy many years ago.

It seems that on a quiet afternoon back in the days of music-hall strippers, two *Times* reporters decided to play hooky from the office and strolled over to one of the Minsky burlesque houses, not far from Times Square. These two reporters, we'll call them Manny and Mike, walked up to the ticket-seller's booth and told the woman inside: "We'd like complimentary tickets, we're newspapermen." "You're what?" she said, taken aback. "We're newspapermen," Manny repeated, pride in his voice. She asked them to wait a minute and dialed a number on her phone. The reporters fidgeted. Suddenly, out of a private elevator emerged the dapper and famous Mr. Minsky himself. Now it was the reporters' turn to be startled. Why had the king of burlesque come all the way down from his penthouse over their routine request for free tickets?

"We didn't mean to trouble you, Mr. Minsky," Mike mumbled.

"No trouble at all," said Minsky, a big smile on his face. "You see, in the burlesque business 'newspapermen' are the guys who slip down into the front rows of the theater to get a close-up view and sit with a newspaper over their laps with their hands underneath it. So I wanted to come down personally to meet the first two guys in all my years who were bold enough to openly announce they were newspapermen."

I felt that this bawdy tale was appropriate to the topic because of all the exotic changes in journalism over the last ten or fifteen years. Sex is a much bigger deal in the reporting world than it used to be. Not so long ago, at least into the mid-1980s, the journalism code under which I was trained was still in effect at mainstream newspapers and radio and television networks. One guiding rule in that code was specifically about covering the private lives of public figures. If you couldn't demonstrate compellingly in your story that the personal conduct in question had a measurable effect on public policy or on the lives of the citizenry, then you didn't write about it. It didn't get published. At least not by those parts of the press that regarded themselves as mainstream.

We thought it was a good rule. At the poker table in the capitol pressroom in Albany, we might joke about the governor's sexual wanderings, but the idea of putting the details on someone's breakfast table seemed nasty. We were reporters; we hadn't signed on to stake out love nests, peer into bedroom windows.

How quaint those days seem. So quaint, in fact, that not only are mainstream media organizations prepared to chronicle extramarital trysts these days, but some have even established actual sex beats. They don't call them sex beats, of course—not yet, anyway—but that's what the reporters are assigned to. Some of the sex reporters have already become famous, and rich. In essence, we have a new species of reporter, and they're in the mainstream. Why not? We have science reporters, political reporters, business reporters, health reporters, consumer affairs reporters, sports reporters. Why not add sex reporters to the mix? Don't be stodgy. Don't squirm and feel tainted. Get jiggy with the sex beat.

Yes, my group is really quaint. So quaint that we are now being scolded by some of the current rulers of journalism. They say we betrayed our sworn duty to hold public officials to the highest moral standards. I find their criticism curious, if not disingenuous. Are they attacking the old standards to divert attention from their absence of standards? For it is not just the rules about privacy that have been thrown out, but virtually all the checks against shoddy reporting. Detailed sourcing is now more often the exception than the norm; analysis and predictions are increasingly being substituted for actual reporting; and it is now deemed acceptable to put stories and gossip from other media outlets on your pages without being able to confirm the accuracy yourself—and without giving any warning to the readers or viewers that this information may be harmful to their grip on the truth.

All this has happened with almost no pause for real debate within the journalistic community. There was plenty of after-the-fact hand-wringing and breast-beating, but mostly just a whimpering, silent surrender by reporters and editors alike to an invisible devil who made them do it. Major editors all over the country, emulating Stepford wives, now seem to intone the same defeated mantra. It goes like this: "We can't help ourselves. There's no time to check the credibility of all these stories pouring out of cable news and the Internet on a round-the-clock basis. But we have to keep up for the sake of our readers, so we include the stories in our reports. We have no choice." When editors announce that they can no longer do their jobs—that is, that they can no longer be the gatekeepers who separate the wheat from the chaff before it's dumped on the public—then is it not fair to ask whether they might not want to seek another career track?

Are there practical steps that journalists and media proprietors can take to stem this negative slide, steps that might keep us from sinking any lower on the scale of public respect? Of course there are, so, having listed some of the problems, let's move to offering concrete ways to turn things around. The biggest step the media could take would be to stop ducking the central issue, the fact that we the press hold accountable every profession, pressure group, institution, and constituency except one: ourselves. We present ourselves as society's watchdog, but we refuse to watch over our own lapses and abuses.

There are roughly fifteen hundred newspapers in this country. Only about fifteen have an ombudsman on the staff to respond to readers' complaints. Even fewer actually have reporters who cover the press, and most of that coverage is business news that appears in the financial pages. Aside from some public broadcast programs, I know of no television or radio news operation that has a reporter whose permanent assignment is to examine the press. When it comes to looking at itself, the watchdog is a lamb, timid and tame. Put simply, the press is afraid to devote the same resources and energy and purpose to covering its own doings that it devotes to everyone else's. What coverage exists is generally soft and superficial and almost never probing.

It's not hard to explain why. The press simply doesn't want to stir up trouble in its own backyard.

The paper that uncovers abuses on some other publication knows it will have to quickly gird for an assault on its own dirty linen. Everyone has closets. Everyone has skeletons.

What would vigorous coverage of the press by the press accomplish? In my view, a lot. I believe it would raise the embarrassment level to a point that could not be tolerated, meaning that media organizations would have to clean up their acts or face public ridicule and maybe the ultimate punishment, loss of audience and advertising.

Beyond the crucial need to report on ourselves the way we report on others, there are many other concrete things we can do to win back public trust. We can start by displaying corrections more prominently. If a page one story was flawed enough to bring the reader to a false conclusion, then write a corrective story and put that on page one, too. Yes, any reporters or editors involved with the story would suffer the pain of embarrassment, but if the policy were applied fairly and equally to all the staff, then my bet is that almost immediately standards on that paper would rise because everyone would be taking greater care to make their stories more complete and error-proof.

The kind of corrections most papers print now deal mostly with minutiae and often sound downright silly. I made this one up, but it's a typical example: "In yesterday's obituary on Freebus Manifold, inventor of wax paper, his wife's name was incorrectly given as Lucy. It is Lucia. Also, their marriage date was given as 1973, instead of 1972."

The most serious mistakes in the press are not about spelling or dates or anything minute. They have to do with such lapses as anonymous sourcing or the failure to seek comment from a central figure in a story or the insertion of opinion into a news story or the omission of information that thereby alters the basic thrust of a story. Only rarely, however, does one see a correction on significant missteps of this kind.

Finally, what about all those thin and poorly sourced items that spew out of the Internet these days and are then inserted, without any fact-checking, into the stories of mainstream papers and network news? Common sense and professional standards both say that unconfirmed stories should be kept off the air and out of print. But we know that in what passes for real life, editors are going to succumb to perceived competitive pressures and shove the stuff into their news reports. So as a stopgap measure, couldn't they at least put a special label on this godawful rubbish, so the reader can see that we are making distinctions between the news we stand by and information that may be raw sewage? My suggestion is that we stick such stuff in the nether regions of the paper under a headline reading: "Stories from Other Outlets That We Were Unable to Confirm."

As the saying goes, don't hold your breath until any of these ideas gets adopted by your favorite newspaper or television network.

By this time you may very well be asking: Who the hell am I to throw down these challenges, to lecture anyone else about press ethics and standards? Am I free of all journalistic sin, perhaps a candidate for media sainthood? Quite the contrary. I am just a reporter who's been in the profession for forty years and made my share, or maybe more than my share, of mistakes. Some of them have been real beauts. I learned my journalistic code essentially from two sources—first, from my mentors in the newsroom of the *New York Times* who carried the scars and wisdom of having covered the Great Depression and World War II, and second, from the lessons of the above-mentioned mistakes. You rarely learn much from your successes; you're too busy celebrating.

Let me digress for a moment and tell you about one of those mistakes. It had to do with the titillating coverage of Nelson Rockefeller's death. It was the late 1970s and I was the city editor of the *Times*. We got the news of his fatal heart attack after the first edition had closed, but put together a passable story for the late editions. As we kept updating the story, we learned that the former governor and vice president hadn't died where his press spokesman said he had died, alone in his office at Rockefeller Center, but instead in a townhouse several blocks away, with his mistress. By the next morning the newsroom was in a state of high excitement. The senior editors were buzzing with adrenaline, telling me we had to surround the story, put as many reporters on it as necessary, get every possible detail of the circumstances of his death. Soon I had caught the fever, too.

For the next week or maybe ten days we ran long stories every day, many of them on page one—naming the woman, describing what she was wearing (a sequined evening dress), reporting that he looked as if he had been dressed hurriedly by someone else after the heart attack. One sock was missing, an emergency-services medic told one of the reporters I had sent out to be relentless. Medics, doormen, neighbors—all were surrounded by my horde. Not surprisingly, the other papers in town were doing the same thing, but this story is about my mistake, not theirs.

How did my editors and I justify the frenzy? Nelson Rockefeller, we told ourselves, was a public figure—no longer governor or vice president but still a public man who exerted an influence on public policy. Since the evidence we dredged up showed that he and the woman had failed to call 911 right away, probably out of a panicked wish not to be discovered in a compromising situation, it was probable that if he hadn't been with his mistress, he would have reacted differently and could have been saved. Then we would still have this public man in our midst, making a public contribution. That's why, we rationalized, we had to report all the lurid details about the mistress, including the apartment he had bought for her down the street from the townhouse where he was found dead with one sock on.

It was, of course, all nonsense. We were pumping up the story because it was about the illicit sex of a famous man. We could never demonstrate, in any of our heavy-breathing articles, that Nelson Rockefeller's death had any public impact outside of the prurient interest we helped generate. Our rationale was nothing more than grand rationalization.

What *should* we have done? First, we should have stayed cool and professional and not allowed ourselves to be tempted by the prurient possibilities. Then we should have covered the story as we would the death of any prominent person. The answer was to give it appropriate coverage, not scandal coverage, not a multiday, front-page extravaganza.

I had grown queasy even before the story finally petered out from its own lack of meaning. This uneasiness kept some of the juicy tidbits we uncovered out of the paper, thank goodness. When the whole thing was over, I knew in my gut it had been a mistake. I also knew that the *New York Times* was not going to publish a page one story saying it had been a mistake, nor would any of the other papers that joined in the mud bath. But that's exactly what we owed our readers, an honest story about how we got caught up in a swirl of excitement, discarded good judgment, and then rationalized ourselves into thinking we had no choice but to run with the illicit-sex story because it was a public service. Sound familiar? Yes, that old reliable justification for everything tawdry—the public's right to know.

I came out of that experience chastened, knowing that the old rule was still a good rule. If private acts have no effect on the public, then they are probably not a story, certainly not a big story, prominently played. It's an honorable rule, and when we have followed it, it has kept us out of the muck and mire we're caught in today.

You may disagree with my point of view, and that's fine, but if you do, if you think there is a new journalism out there that has made obsolete the curious artifact now being described as the old journalism, then I believe an obligation falls on you to explain to the public what this new journalism consists of, what its rules are, or, indeed, if it has any rules. You must make a compelling case for its validity. You must demonstrate persuasively how, under this new journalism, its practitioners deserve to be called professionals with honor and not just averagely educated casual labor on floating pickup teams of windbags and scribblers. You cannot simply announce that the old rules are dead without replacing them with something you can at least explain—that is, with a new journalistic contract that the community will respect. Otherwise you will merely be saying that henceforth there are no guidelines, no strictures, no limits. In other words, the credo of this new journalism is: Anything goes. You will simply put all possible information out there for the public—gossip, rumors, advocacy journalism, sex stories, wild reporting, solid reporting—put it all in the same stewpot, and let the public decide what it wants to believe.

For myself, there is no old or new journalism. There is only good journalism and flawed journalism. A well-reported story will always be a well-reported story. Thucydides' *Peloponnesian War,* written around 400 B.C., was well reported; it is still well reported. Go read it. Go read Homer Bigart's dispatches from World War II. Go read A. J. Liebling's collected works entitled *The Wayward Press.* If that's the old journalism, let it revel in being called old.

In truth, the only new things in journalism are the computer-driven tools for gathering information and transmitting news. Simply put, we can get news faster and in greater quantities now because of the technology revolution. But a good story is still a good story. It must be carefully and rigorously reported before it can be delivered to the public as news. Only then can you plug in the new toys and send the story across the world in a nanosecond.

Am I saying that there is very little good journalism being done today in America? Absolutely not. I began in newspapering believing that journalism was a useful calling, sometimes even a noble one. Discouraged as I may be by the current landscape, my belief in the merit of journalism has not changed. I know that a lot of fine journalism shows up on a regular basis all over the country. Every time I get involved as a judge in one of the journalism contests, I see firsthand the great stuff. It energizes me. There's as much purpose and passion among young journalists today as there has ever been. The problem is, more and more often, the good work gets bypassed or overshadowed or drowned out by a product emanating from our so-called media capitals that is best described as noise posing as journalism. Sometimes, pornography posing as journalism. This isn't just about the Clinton-Lewinsky story. This has been building for many years.

Let's go back to one of the benchmark events in our ever-accelerating downward journey. I refer to the historic weekend in 1987 when the *Miami Herald* staked out Gary Hart's townhouse in Washington to play Peeping Tom and catch him with Donna Rice, a young woman not his wife. Within a week, Hart had been destroyed as a candidate for the Democratic nomination for president and walked off into political oblivion.

The *Herald* justified its stakeout by saying that Hart, responding to rumors of womanizing, had dared the press to follow him around. Hart had said: "Follow me around. I don't care. I'm serious. If anybody wants to put a tail on me, go ahead. They'd be very bored." But that challenge was made to a *New York Times* reporter who was interviewing Hart for a magazine profile and it did not appear in print until the Sunday of the fateful weekend. Which means that the *Herald* knew nothing about it when the reporters set up their ambush. I criticized the surveillance in my opinion column at the time and I remember including an astonishing comment by Michael Gartner, then head of NBC News and the immediate past president of the American Society of Newspaper Editors. Normally a coherent man, Gartner praised the *Herald's* work as "one of democracy's finest hours" and "just a wonderful thing for America." He was right about one thing. It was indeed historic—sadly historic.

We've come a long way from that finest hour. We have marched forward with bigger and better stings and ambushes by brave journalists who see it as their divinely ordained mission to confront public officials with such questions as: "Are you now or have you ever been an adulterer?" I can't believe that most journalists are comfortable with being the sex police. And if they're not comfortable with it, if they feel demeaned by it, then why are they participating in it? Why aren't reporters saying no to such assignments? Why aren't they shouting at editors and proprietors that they won't allow the profession to sink any lower into the ooze?

I've asked these questions of groups of journalists and I usually get either silence or some very practical responses. "How can I do that without getting fired? . . . I have to support my family," the journalists say.

I can't tell anybody that they should forfeit their job. But at the same time, I know that when bad things are happening and the people closest to them don't speak up, then the bad things will get worse. That's what we have seen vividly happening in the

Clinton-Lewinsky scandal. Page one stories, based on pure speculation, saying that the president went out in public wearing a necktie that Monica Lewinsky had given him so he could send her a signal, sort of a message of solidarity to influence her testimony before Kenneth Starr's grand jury. Trouble is, while he and the tie were in the Rose Garden being televised, Lewinsky—as the whole world had been told—was testifying before that very grand jury, behind closed doors, no outsiders allowed in to bring messages and no way for her to see the tie on television in time to have it affect her testimony. Any neophyte police reporter could have spotted the holes in that story and saved the editors the embarrassment of running it. Or maybe they weren't embarrassed. That's what a raging fever will do to you.

Are we the press comfortable with this? I don't think so. But we're not doing much about it either, except forming a few committees and cutting down a lot of trees to issue long reports about how many times the major papers printed stories using fewer than two sources to back them up. *We don't need any more reports.* We need to *do something* about the problem. Because it has tainted us—all of us, not just those writing about thong underwear and the shape of the president's penis.

I've heard all the arguments that seek to justify this squalid coverage. None impresses me. There have always been at least two tiers of journalism in this country, the gossip press and the mainstream press. I see nothing wrong with that. The human species has always relished a dose of nasty gossip about someone else. It makes us feel better about our own mottled lives. In the past, these citizens would go to the gossip press for rumors and sex scandals. For responsible news, they went to the mainstream press.

Now, it would seem, the two are merging. Mainstream publications are adopting, more and more, the role of the penny press, the supermarket tabloids, the movie-gossip magazines. There are some mainstream holdouts, but their numbers are dwindling. It would take a real fight to get us back to the two-tier system. And the fight will have to come from within. From reporters and editors and the media proprietors. No one else can clean our stable. It was we who made the mess. We who threw out the rules. We who made up the rationalizations. We will therefore have to wield the mops and buckets.

My friend and colleague Russell Baker has put it as well as anyone ever will. In a column not long ago, he said: "Who will ever again want to become a journalist? Imagine, mother, do you want that lovely little child of yours to grow up and spend a long, malodorous life writing stories that make you shudder with disgust?

"The Watergate journalists Woodward and Bernstein inspired a whole generation of young people to think of journalism as an honorable way to spend a life. That is the generation that's now trying to look solemn instead of leering and winking as it issues the daily bulletins on ladies' dirty linen. These wretched media people know it's filthy work, but somebody, they say, has to do it, just as somebody has to clean septic tanks. What pious baloney."

He's absolutely right. Members of the Washington press corps keep saying the story revolts them and yet every day they dive right back into the muck. Mainstream papers, for example, are still planning to send out the same questionnaires to presidential candidates for the election in 2000 that they sent out the last time, questionnaires that include questions about their sex lives. If media leaders are feeling embarrassment, it's not showing up in their actions.

How do we tell our children about all this, about what profession we're in, and about how it lost adult supervision and went out of control, along with the president, the special investigator, and the Congress? What if your teenage child listens carefully as you describe the work of the press and then says: "Could *your* sex life stand public scrutiny in transcript form?" How will the obituaries of the reporters on the sex beat read in the days to come? Will such an obit begin: "Michael Isikoff, press-winning illicit-sex reporter, died today etcetera etcetera." Or, "Chris Matthews, successful television talk-show host who specialized in adultery and other sexual topics, passed over today and so on." You laugh, but maybe I'm not that far off.

Finally, I'd like to bring us back to the ideas mentioned earlier—in particular to the notion that every large newspaper and every radio and television network should provide regular coverage of the press, the same kind of detailed, specialized coverage we apply to government, politics, business, medicine, and the law. I don't think the average consumer of news realizes how revolutionary an idea this is. Maybe it's because he or she has been conditioned to see the press examine everything but the press and has unconsciously come to accept that as the norm. It's a norm so hypocritical that it should leap out at all of us. For the press to hold everyone accountable but itself defies all logic. It also defies the tenets of honesty and candor that the press says it is committed to, not to mention its promise to cover all subjects "without fear or favor," no matter how unpleasant the task.

If we really want to restore our credibility, we will have to look at ourselves and do it in public. I'm not talking about covering the press as a business story in the financial section. I'm talking about covering the press as a powerful institution, about demystifying ourselves to the reader and viewer, about describing the process of how we gather information, how we screen it and check it before putting it in the public domain—or how we don't check it properly sometimes, meaning we would actually tell the reader about our stumbles and embarrassments. We would not wrap ourselves in a cloak of purity, but instead create a commonality with our public by saying that we, too, like you, are fallible. I think people respect you when you stop posing as a God-king and reveal yourself as mortal flesh. I truly believe this is the best chance we have to shore up journalism's traditional standards. And, no, I don't think it will be easy.

I know this from personal experience. For the last three years, after I resigned from *Newsday* when the parent company, Times Mirror, shut it down for stock-price reasons, I have spent much of my time trying to persuade mainstream press institutions to embrace the idea of covering the press in the same way they cover everything else. I went to every name news organization I could think of, leaving out only the few who already had an ombudsman or at least some respectable form of press coverage. I went to newspapers, magazines, all the networks. Their responses will make a great chapter in my memoirs. Everyone said it was a great idea, but everyone also came up with some pesky reason why it couldn't be done.

Naturally I was disappointed. But not exactly surprised. Nor discouraged. In the end, the fight will have to be waged over time, from within, by reporters and editors willing to risk disfavor or worse by insisting on quality journalism. No outsider is going to do this for us. We can't be passive.

We in the press talk constantly about how the lifeblood of democracy is the free and honest flow of information. Please note that the key word is information, not sludge. As a colleague of mine said recently: “The phrase ‘drive-by’ is supposed to describe the crime, not the coverage.” The First Amendment doesn’t exempt journalists from the need to be responsible. It’s our house. No one else can clean it but us.

7.

What Is Missing From Your News?

By Jay Harris

At the country's beginnings, most newspapers and magazines were run by one person, or one family, who served as the reporters, the business managers, and the printers rolled into one. As journalism became bigger and bigger business, the jobs were separated, and the preferred policy was to keep the advertising and circulation departments sharply away from the editorial side, so that reporting the news would not be swayed by financial considerations. Talk about full circle: One of the biggest complaints of journalists and press critics today is that the walls of separation have fallen, and that money is driving decisions on what is news.

Although Jay Harris is a publisher himself, with substantial experience in the business operations of magazines, he freely agrees with the criticism and laments the effects on the workings of democracy. Of course, his position is somewhat unique. Since 1991 he has worked for Mother Jones, *a progressive magazine founded in 1976 and devoted to reporting stories that the rest of the press overlooks. The magazine is supported with some advertising revenue, but more from subscriptions and donations. That gives Harris uncommon freedom to explain how journalism really works.*

Before joining Mother Jones, *Harris was general manager of* Newsweek*'s Pacific operations, publisher of the Asia edition of* Travel & Leisure, *and director of special projects for* Newsweek International. *The award-winning* Mother Jones *magazine is named after Mary Harris "Mother" Jones, a pioneer U.S. labor organizer and radical agitator.*

It's kind of risky for a guy like me to be associated with journalists. The polling puts the journalism profession somewhere south of politicians, lawyers, and used car salesmen in the public esteem. You can look it up: a mid-90s Gallup poll found that the number of Americans who rate journalists highly in terms of ethics and honesty was a whopping 22 percent.

To bolster my credibility, I want to assure you that I'm from the other side of the publishing industry. I'm from the pragmatic workaday class of publishing-business people: the folks who suffer through long lunches at fancy restaurants with advertising clients so as to keep the lights turned on and those ungrateful, overspending, deadline-pushing scribblers paid. Compared to the tortured souls of the journalists, our mission is crystal-clear. Next quarter's profits up? Good. Down? Bad. It's very, very clear. You can trust me. I'm an MBA.

I'm being flip, of course. But because the demands of business are so much of what is driving the content of our news today, and because I've seen those firsthand during my nine years at *Newsweek,* inside the Washington Post Corporation, and watched the pressures accelerate during my years at *Mother Jones,* I believe I have something to add. So let me talk from the perspective of a businessperson and of a citizen about what is missing from our news. I want to get into some of the specific stories you aren't seeing, offer some observations about how journalism came to this point and what that means for our society, and then speak briefly about what we can do to redress the gaping information holes in our most-read, most-watched news media.

Before I get there, let me tell you just a little about *Mother Jones.* We are a modest-size, independent, nonprofit magazine and website based in San Francisco. Our editors, and the journalists who write for us, have well-tuned, highly sensitive crap detectors and share, with a lot of other people in this country, a deep sense of democratic outrage at injustice, hypocrisy, dangerous practice, and out-and-out criminality by people in power. We hold to the somewhat old-fashioned notion that a free press can and should help hold that power in account. So at *Mother Jones* we specialize in reporting that looks behind the facades of political and corporate and media power and reports back to let the rest of us know what is going on. We take special delight in stories that take the air out of dangerous political gasbags and corporate criminals. We also like to connect the dots of smaller news items into broad and important stories. And, since "important" journalism can too often appear stuffy and inaccessible—eat your vegetables—we work to make it appetizing. We seek to create a magazine with style, with good writing and cool design, ample humor, and a broad spectrum of stories. For those with a reporting jones, there is nothing more rewarding than work at *Mother Jones*. But here is the catch: *Mother Jones* is not sizzling swimsuit supermodels, treacly homage to Diana, or tips on better sex, faster weight loss, and great vacation spots. Our kind of publishing loses money.

To produce a different kind of magazine, we've had to set up a different way of staying in business. Our financial formula is quite distinct from that of 99 percent of the news media in the country. To be freed from some of the pressures that journalists working in advertising-driven, commercial news operations face, *Mother Jones* was set up as a nonprofit. We do carry advertising—in fact, a part of my job is to help sell potential advertisers on the value of our smart, cranky, don't-bullshit-me readers. But advertising accounts for only about 15 percent of our revenue, as opposed to 50 percent for a typical commercial magazine. Overall, we're a lot more like community radio than a typical ad-driven magazine. Our books are kept in balance by subscriptions and contributions from readers and a small number of foundations. Budgets are perennially tight, but there is an overriding virtue: The editors aren't editing to deliver a profit. They're editing to deliver the news.

In contrast, most newspeople today are employees of giant entertainment companies, corporations whose stock is publicly traded, who report quarterly profits to Wall Street, whose executives—including, often, top editorial people—are compensated with stock options and profit-triggered bonuses. In the media business today there is relentless pressure to be profitable. True, the notion that journalism has a role to help the public keep informed and make reasoned judgments as citizens is a spark that hasn't been completely tamped out. But day in, day out, in thousands of decisions small and large, the pressure to be profitable, to advance within the organization, to please the boss, earn the bonus, keep up with the competition affects the information reported by these companies.

Let me juxtapose that with how pervasive the information products of these companies are, using the numbers of Robert McChesney, an author and media watcher. The biggest multinational media and entertainment conglomerate is Time Warner. The company's 1997 sales were twenty-four billion dollars, bigger than the gross domestic product of many small countries. What does Time Warner own? For starters, magazines: *Time, Life, People, Money, Sports Illustrated, Entertainment Weekly, Fortune, Parenting, Health, Sunset, Southern Living*—in all, twenty-four of our biggest, and several of our most influential, magazines. It owns several U.S. and global cable television channels, including CNN, Headline News, TBS, TNT, Turner Classic Movies, and CNN-SI, a cross-production with *Sports Illustrated.* It owns HBO and Cinemax, partly owns Comedy Central, and has a controlling stake in Court TV. It has the second-largest cable system in the United States, controlling the cable monopolies in twenty-two of the largest one hundred markets. It owns Warner Brothers and New Line Cinema film studios. It controls more than one thousand movie screens outside the United States. It owns a library of six thousand films, twenty-five thousand television programs, and a huge back-list of book titles, recorded music, and cartoons. Its various book publishing operations would, if combined, form the second-largest book publishing business in the world. Time Warner also controls the Warner Music Group, one of the largest global music businesses. And it owns 50 percent of DC Comics—Batman, Superman, and over sixty other titles.

I mention the heroes of DC Comics to distinguish them from the owners of Mickey Mouse and Donald Duck. That would be, of course, Disney/CapCities/ABC, the second-largest global media entertainment conglomerate. Disney's 1997 sales were twenty-two billion dollars, its profits two billion dollars, and it controls: ABC television (223 affiliated stations) and the ABC radio network (with twenty-nine hundred affiliated stations); ten U.S. major-market TV stations and twenty-one U.S. radio stations; several major film and television production studios; the Disney Channel, ESPN, ESPN2, and ESPNews; part of Lifetime, part of A&E; and also book and magazine publishing, music, theme parks, and more than five hundred Disney stores.

Then there's Bertlesmann (fifteen billion dollars in 1997 revenues), Viacom (thirteen billion dollars), Rupert Murdoch's News Corporation (ten billion dollars plus), and General Electric, a media company by virtue of its ownership of NBC and its partnership with Microsoft in MSNBC. I could go on, but you get my point.

Where's the news? Oh, it's there all right. Certainly the news operations are there—on your TV sets, on the newsstands, and, most significantly perhaps, on financial spreadsheets around the planet showing contribution margins and audience ratings. But the profit yardstick being used to measure the "success" of news operations is only indirectly related to anything that might be called the public interest. In fact, it runs almost completely contrary to our historical notion of a watchdog press. That very simple fact has a huge impact on the news we see.

These companies aren't going to change their priorities. The company directors are legally obliged to manage for profit. It's up to the rest of us, as consumers of the news, to challenge the notion that the quest for more eyeballs at lower cost around the clock is serving the public's need to know, is justifying the licenses we grant for the use of public airwaves and to the cable monopolies, is justifying the protection we give the press under the First Amendment. If money, rather than some notion of the public good, is driving the news, then let's follow the money and see what it is squeezing out of our media diet.

Let me try to be fair to what history tells us: Entertainment has always been part of the news business. William Randolph Hearst and Joseph Pulitzer amassed fortunes on the strength of celebrity, crisis, and scandal. You may have heard about the famous telegram sent one hundred years ago during the Spanish-American War from the *New York World* editor to his correspondent in Cuba. "Send all the details," the cable read. "Never mind the facts." We all like a good soap opera and if it's filled with real-life heroes and villains, so much the better.

There was a time, though, not that far past, when newspapers and even most broadcast outlets were largely local affairs. Ownership was, if not necessarily enlightened, at least dispersed and often resident in, and thus at least mildly accountable to, the hometown. There was a time, too, when broadcast news programming in radio and TV was somewhat shielded from the pressure to deliver big audiences at all costs. That was in part due to the terms of the licenses granted by the Federal Communications Commission to broadcasters, which required a certain amount of news programming, and in part due to the fact that the broadcasters themselves hadn't figured out how to make much money from the news. Even in the early 1980s, when greed was good and consolidation in the media business was accelerating, restrictions on cross-ownership of different media in the same markets kept "synergy" at bay. The sellout of the news hadn't reached warp speed.

Then came O. J. The O. J. Simpson story—scandal, celebrity, race, and true crime all rolled together—was enormously profitable for all the news shows, but perhaps most especially for CNN, which covered the scandal from all angles for large portions of every day. The programming was cheap. The stars and the script were free, and a young company could simply put its reporting resources out in Los Angeles to catch the manna falling from the Hollywood firmament. The ratings were astronomical. And because there was sure to be a next installment, the marketers could have a field day pulling audiences to the cliffhanger, selling advertisers record numbers of viewers.

We saw it again with the media orgy around the death of Princess Diana. The brass woke up. There's gold here. Reality shows had always been cheap programming to keep the ads from banging together. Now it turned out they could pull blockbuster ratings, too.

To give a sense of what the chase for ratings does to the news, I want to quote from an interview of Dan Rather done by Steven Brill for an issue of *Brill's Content* in the fall of 1998. Brill asked Rather what he would dream to see happen with the *CBS Evening News.* He even prods Rather along, asking what if there were no ratings. Rather talks about going to a full hour of news, expanding the international news hole, getting away from "if it bleeds, it leads." Not bad. I could get behind that.

So Brill asks who makes the decision about what gets on the *CBS Evening News.* "Me," Rather replied. "I'm the managing editor."

So, Brill said, "You're the guy who decided on July 29 that the demolition of O. J. Simpson's house on Rockingham was more important than thousands of people being killed on [the flooding] Yangtze River [in China]? . . . Tell me how that decision got made."

Rather answered with some waffle about deciding to put the Yangtze story later in the show so maybe they could pick up more time for it. But why run the O. J. story at all, Brill asked. Why not give all the time to the China story?

And Rather answered: "Fear." He went on: "Fear runs strong in every newsroom in the country right now, a lot of fears, but one fear is common—the fear that if we don't do it, they will get a few more readers, a few more listeners, a few more viewers than we do."

"The Hollywoodization of the news," Rather said, "is deep and abiding."

Remember, when that interview took place, the Monica story was just getting warmed up.

For the better part of 1998 and well into 1999, we

had Lewinsky/Clinton mesmerizing editors, producers, most media gatekeepers, and—despite polls saying "enough already"—a hell of a lot of the rest of us. How much of this coverage brought out facts that might reasonably be considered relevant to the "constitutional crisis" provoked by President Clinton's behavior, and how much was about ratings? Consider that the Barbara Walters interview with Monica Lewinsky in March 1999, drew the second-largest TV ratings of the year, right behind the Super Bowl. MSNBC, the most extreme of the all-Monica, all-the-time news providers, saw its rating plummet after the impeachment vote finally clanged the lid down on the Monica saga. Let's face it, from the consumer end there was a fair amount of social pressure to keep up with the soap opera. You show up at class the day after Kenneth Starr's report was released and not get the cigar jokes? You're a bozo. Love Clinton or hate him, this frenzy was largely about a blockbuster national melodrama that swamped even the movie *Titanic*.

Trouble is, this soap opera, and all the other reality shows designed to deliver our frontal lobes to eager advertisers, crowd out a huge range of stories on the quality of lives we lead, the jobs we work at, the safety of the food we eat, the quality of the schools we attend or send our kids to.

Let me get to some specifics. For starters, go back with me now to February 19, 1996. It is President's Day, and Monica Lewinsky has been summoned to the Oval Office. According to his grand jury testimony, Bill Clinton no longer felt right about their intimate relationship, and he had to put a stop to it. Later, in the summer of 1998, Lewinsky testified to the grand jury that, during their meeting, Clinton placed a return call to a person who was later identified as Alfonso Fanjul, a Florida sugar magnate and mega campaign donor to both Republicans and Democrats. Fanjul's call came in to the White House at 12:24 P.M. Twelve minutes later, the president of the United States, leader of the free world, returned Fanjul's call. He and Fanjul spoke for twenty-two minutes, an eternity in presidential time.

Who is this man with the president's phone number and why would he be calling the Oval Office on a federal holiday? We don't know what Clinton and Fanjul discussed, but, with a modest search of contemporary news reports, *Mother Jones*'s editor turned up the following facts that suggest some possible topics of their chitchat. Earlier that day in 1996, at a press conference in the Everglades, Vice President Al Gore had proposed a penny-per-pound tax on sugar, a tax to be earmarked for the restoration of the Everglades, polluted by years of sugar-cane runoff. Later that same week, it turns out, the House of Representatives was to vote on a measure to repeal sugar price supports, a subsidy worth $1.4 billion per year to sugar producers, and worth a tidy $65 million a year to Fanjul's companies.

Let's look at that measure to repeal sugar price

supports. Free marketers should like it because it helps get the government out of subsidizing private business. Big companies like Coke and Hershey should like it because it lowers the cost of a major ingredient. Environmentalists should like it because growing sugar cane near the Everglades is an environmental disaster. Liberals should like it because it lowers the cost of a consumer staple. The lead sponsor of the bill is a Republican from Florida, and the Republicans control the House. It seems a laugher: Kiss that subsidy goodbye.

So how come the bill is defeated 217-208? The White House offered no support for the repeal of sugar price supports. Speaker Newt Gingrich, Mr. "Let's-End-Big-Government," withheld his support. At the last minute, even a few Democrats and Republicans who had sponsored the measure shifted and voted against it. As for the penny-per-pound tax? The Clinton administration quietly let that proposal morph into a Florida ballot initiative that was whacked at the polls after the sugar industry spent millions to defeat it.

Could these warped results have anything to do with the fact that in the 1995–1996 election cycle, the Fanjul family and its associates pumped more than nine hundred thousand dollars into the election system? Here is a news story: Washington is so up to its ears in institutional bribery that a no-brainer reform gets sold out to a couple of Sugar Daddies with Spanish passports. And us schmoes who can't even read about this scam in our local newspaper? We're not only in the dark, we're footing the bill. Corporate welfare in the form of entitlements buried in the tax codes will cost taxpayers nearly four trillion dollars between 1996 and 2003. Meanwhile, the tax burden is shifting to guess who? The assets of the richest 5 percent of Americans have doubled over the past two decades while the real income of the rest of us has declined. In short, we are witnessing a transfer of wealth from the many to the few the likes of which haven't been seen since the days of the nineteenth-century robber barons. Why isn't the press covering it?

To be fair, in April 1999—some seven months after the *Mother Jones* story—the *New York Times* put its version on the front page under the headline, "Sugar Industry's Pivotal Role in Everglades Effort." It was a typically solid *Times* story, going into fair detail about the environmental situation and specifically citing the Fanjul call interrupting the president's meeting with Monica *S.* Lewinsky. (Don't you love it when the *Times* does that? It gives you the impression that any publication so thorough, so buttoned-up that it would go to the trouble to stick the "S." in Monica's name *every* time, would never leave out anything important. Only it did.)

Though the *Times* story mentioned, in passing, the sugar price support program and even quoted the sponsor of the bill saying that Alfonso Fanjul was a powerful player, it neglected to mention what this corporate welfare program means personally to the Fanjuls or to the rest of us, who are not only picking up the tab for higher sugar prices at the grocery store, but also are now about to fund, through our tax dollars, some Rube Goldberg system of pumps and dikes and storage tanks to deal with seasonal floodwaters because, thanks to our subsidy, it is still profitable to grow sugar near the Everglades.

Take note: Some things are missing from your *New York Times*. For all the news it sees fit to print, it appears that expecting the newspaper of record for the power elite to explain in plain language the impact of a corporate subsidy for the rest of us is like expecting pigs to fly. Maybe the publisher would suffer nasty stares over his frisée at the club. Possibly it was seen by the editor as unseemly to offer too many specifics of how crudely political power is wielded. More likely, it might complicate the paper's intertwined business-cum-news-source relationships with a variety of political players. The truth is, I don't know how the *Times* got so tantalizingly close to this important, connect-the-dots kind of point, and then whiffed it.

I do know what contortions the *Times* and others go through to explain to *Mother Jones* that what we keep digging up isn't news. It's a problem of getting our kind of news picked up. Take the example of a recent *Mother Jones* story called "Planted Hollywood." You see, the U.S. Forest Service has this problem: Most Americans, when driving through their national forests, want to see trees. If, instead of trees, taxpayers see clear-cuts from logging operations, they tend to get all emotional and unreasonable. They start demanding that it stop, start wondering loudly how it was allowed to happen. This puts a bind on a lot of the tax-funded employees at our Forest Service, who believe that their job is to help timber companies cut down the trees in the national forests. What to do, what to do?

Turns out, high technology has come to the rescue. Using three million dollars' worth of very sophisticated computer software, the Forest Service can now keep everyone happy, or at least keep the timber folks happy and the rest of us in the dark. Spiffy new geographic information system technology allows the Forest Service to determine exactly where to cut and where to put logging roads so as to hide the destruction from public view. Clear-cuts can be hidden with ridges and "beauty strips," narrow stands of trees maintained to block drivers' views. "Once we've decided we're going to (log), why don't we make it as aesthetically pleasing as we can?" asked Terry Daniel, the head of—get this—the Environmental *Perception* Laboratory at the University of Arizona.

Mother Jones, seeking publicity for the magazine as well as for this outrageous story, pitched it to a number of bigger news organizations. To date, no joy. "It's not news," we've been told. The most positive response: one reporter who said, "Well, maybe the next time I'm doing a story on the Forest Service." Ooooh. I won't turn off my TV until then.

Another excuse we hear a lot of: It's not simple enough. A couple of years ago we were working with the producers of *Inside Edition,* the syndicated TV newsmagazine, providing them with *Mother Jones* stories they could use for their five-nights-a-week show. One time we pitched them on picking up our story of Freeport McMoran's gold-mining operations in Irian Jaya, a remote and primitive part of Indonesia. It's a pretty simple story. This mining company discovered gold in huge amounts and cut a deal with the Indonesian government: We'll give you a nice piece of the action and do all the work and all you have to do is use your army to keep the natives, your citizens, in line when they get uppity about all the tailings being dumped in their water. By the way, let's use your army to help keep the international press entirely out of our operations, too. This mountaintop removal can get pretty ugly. *Inside Edition*'s response was polite but perplexed: "How are you going to get Ma and Pa America to care about Irian Jaya?"

When I get an answer like that about a story as straightforward as that, it not only tells me that the game is about ratings, it makes me boggle about the ability of our media to handle something that actually is complex. For instance, here's a story that I believe could use some news attention: How might we as a nation start to break the cycle of poverty that has trapped millions of poor families and is perpetuating itself at huge human, social, and financial costs?

Some things about that story are very stark: for instance, the stats showing the United States as a world leader in homicide and incarceration rates. The fact that, in Illinois, it costs about sixteen thousand dollars a year to keep an adult in prison versus forty-two hundred a year to keep a child in school. In his book *Children in Jeopardy,* Irving Harris says that for every dollar the State of Illinois spends on prevention—that is, in helping poor kids and poor families stay together, keep healthy, get food, stay in school—it spends one thousand dollars on intervention programs made necessary because it failed to prevent a problem.

Here's the kicker: There are dozens, if not hundreds, of trial programs that are known to be cost-effective in dealing with these very costly problems. There are no panaceas. Some people are helped. Some fall back. Some cheat the programs intended to help them. Politicians and social-service agencies can overstate both the good and the bad. Shouldn't our media help the rest of us evaluate all that? But complexity? Shades of gray? Stories that require thought? How are you going to sell *that* to Ma and Pa America?

Concern about ratings drives many news decisions, but the other part of the profit equation weighs heavily on the news as well. Let's look at advertising, the economic engine of the commercial media world. Despite frequent assertions of vigorous separation of church and state by the solons of the news biz (that's industry-speak for keeping editors independent of business pressures), the pandering to advertisers in the news media can sometimes be absolutely blatant. Go back, for instance, to the early 1960s, when the U.S. surgeon general first declared smoking a health hazard, and track the coverage of tobacco-related issues by the major newsweeklies and the major women's service magazines through the late 1980s, a good twenty-five years. In magazines that devote a substantial number of pages to health-related topics, you'll see shockingly little coverage of the links between smoking and disease. Smoking is still killing four hundred thousand Americans a year and, if all you read was *Cosmo,* you'd think that cellulite had ruined more lives. It's simple: tobacco advertising, particularly after being banned from television, was, and is, a huge ad category for the biggest and most influential American magazines. The word from cigarette sponsors was clear: Don't mess with us or we'll pull our ads. So tobacco went missing from our news.

Big Auto is a bully, too. Consider a now-legendary memo circulated by Chrysler's ad agency. In order to avoid potential conflicts, the letter stated, "It is required that Chrysler Corporation be alerted in advance of any and all editorial content that encompasses sexual, political, or social issues, or any editorial that might be construed as provocative or offensive." The company asked that all media seeking Chrysler's advertising agree to those terms. According to the company, everyone signed.

Let's not leave out Big Oil. Roger Cohn, *Mother*

Jones's new editor in chief, was formerly executive editor at *Audubon* magazine. Seems that as he and the *Audubon* editor started to shift the magazine from a pretty, but fluffy, nature magazine to an attractive and substantial magazine of environmental reporting, they started to run afoul (no bird joke intended) of big Audubon Society donors who did not like criticism of, for instance, Bill Clinton's environmental record. Further, big corporate backers of Audubon, like Phillips Petroleum, thought *Audubon*'s coverage on the problems of waste oil pits in Texas to be in extremely bad taste. Do companies with spotty environmental records try to co-opt media to help with a greenwash? Companies do. The Audubon Society fired the editor in chief and Cohn left. He is safe now; he's with *Mother Jones.*

As we look at the pressure from advertisers and its relatively obvious effects, it is important to realize that there are many more subtle examples of media companies' warping coverage to be consistent with their financial interests.

Let me illustrate. In April 1999, during the Kosovo war, Bill Clinton spoke to the American Society of Newspaper Editors in San Francisco. Among other things, he portrayed the Kosovars as unwitting victims caught between high-tech weaponry and centuries-old ethnic conflict. What you don't hear is that the Clinton administration is the biggest exporter of high-tech weaponry ever. American arms exports have been the cornerstone of the Clinton Commerce

Department's trade strategy—they have doubled since the Bush presidency. Someday soon, if it hasn't happened already, when we decide to be globo-cop in some other part of the world, we will have armed the forces we're fixing to fight. Where is that story, besides on the *Mother Jones* website, the MoJo Wire?

What about this story: Concern about genetic engineering of food crops is a huge issue overseas. There is widespread, scientifically justified concern about the technology itself: the ability of implanted genes to "drift" into surrounding plant life; the safety of genetically altered food crops; the safety of the milk produced by dairy cows shot up with synthetic growth hormones. Then there is concern and anger about the pace of change, about the sellout of the basic building blocks of life to large corporations. Even people who are broadly familiar with this issue can be stunned to learn how fast genetically altered crops are becoming the standard in agriculture. According to *Rachel's Environment and Health Weekly,* in 1997, about 15 percent of the U.S. soybean crop was grown from genetically engineered seed. By the year 2000, considerably more than half of U.S. soybeans will be genetically engineered.

Despite these concerns, and in fact fueling them, official U.S. public policy is to turn a blind eye. No public records need be kept of which farms are using genetically engineered seed. No producers are required to label any crops. The companies that buy from farmers are not required to keep genetically modified crops separate from traditional crops, so purchasers have no way of knowing what they're getting or of avoiding genetically altered crops. Overseas, meanwhile, Indian farmers are burning genetically modified crops in the fields. German ports are turning back shiploads of American grain that contain genetically modified crops. Bonnie Prince Charles has taken the policies of Tony Blair's government to task for being deaf to these concerns.

Where's the American press? Here's what *Time* had to say on February 1, 1999: "For farmers hoping for a healthy harvest, the best place to turn for help these days is the Monsanto Corporation. One of the world's leading biotechnology companies—and lately a pioneer in genetically engineered seed—Monsanto has been incorporating flashy traits like herbicide and pest resistance into everything from canola to corn." The *Time* article goes on to categorize the farmer and consumer outrage over this as "doomsday alarms" from environmentalists.

Here's another big issue that has gotten scant media attention. The Telecommunications Act of 1996 was the most sweeping telecommunications legislation in sixty years. It swept away the fairness doctrine and opened the gates to enormous consolidation of ownership in both radio and TV. Within a year of the bill's passage the nation's top four radio broadcasters (CBS, Clear Channel Communications, Capstar Broadcasting, and ABC Radio) controlled 90 percent of the radio industry's ad revenues. Yet, according to the *Tyndall Report,* which tracks network newscasts, neither the passage of the act nor the signing of it made the top ten stories of those weeks.

What have you read or heard lately in the commercial press about global warming? About Wall Street's multimillion-dollar lobbying campaign to privatize Social Security? Did you know about the larding of the minimum-wage bill with tax breaks to industry?

How to explain the absence of these stories and dozens more like them in scope and significance from the press? Bullying advertisers aren't a complete explanation: Monsanto and the defense contractors do advertise, but their advertising presence in mass media, broadcast or print, is fairly limited. The obsession with ratings doesn't fully explain the blackout either. Certainly even a very responsible take on the unregulated spread of genetically modified crops, through farms and food shelves, could, if properly done, draw socko ratings. Shy of a global news conspiracy, a Trilateral Commission for the News—shy of that, how to explain what's missing from the news?

There is, I think, a "master narrative" at work. The narrative that constrains the news is not scripted from the top by a cabal of corporate owners, but evolves organically, with often eerie cohesion, from a dozen factors common to the corporate news world. The master narrative is part ignorance, part arrogance, part bias, part laziness, and part the economic self-interest of media owners, publishers, editors, and aspiring reporters. As eyeballs are chased, profits reported, and promotions and bonuses announced, as the cultural barriers between editors and key corporate sources fall, as competition is bought out, as business synergies between news and entertainment are sought, a news channel of least resistance is dredged. Short of a crisis, it's damned hard to change the course of that river.

I don't call this self-censorship. That seems far too dainty, too limited a term. But if you think you're getting the whole truth when you read your daily newspaper or flip on the tube for the evening news, think again. Because what you don't know can hurt you.

I want to offer some thoughts about what to do about this fine pickle, but before I do that I will paint the picture just one bit darker. I want to speak about the censorship of paid advertising—that is, the ability of corporate media gatekeepers to keep even paid messages off the airwaves if they find them contrary to their "standards and practices."

According to Lawrence Soley, writing in *Extra!,* the publication of Fairness and Accuracy in reporting, a media watchdog organization, stations in the Minneapolis–St. Paul area refused to sell commercial time to the Prairie Island Sioux for a commercial critical of a plan by Northern States Power to store spent nuclear fuel rods on an island in the middle of the Mississippi. In Detroit, radio stations refused to sell commercial time to the United Auto Workers, which was calling for a boycott of Hudson department stories after a union intimidation campaign by the company. When Jim Hightower's ABC radio network show was dumped after signing up 150 markets, ABC said the show wasn't producing sufficient ad revenue. Before that decision, the network had refused to accept two hundred and fifty thousand dollars of union advertising.

Mother Jones had some related experience with ABC before it canceled Hightower's show. Because Hightower's content was such a good fit with our own, MoJo wanted to advertise. Paid. We don't have the money to do much advertising, but this seemed like a rare opportunity. We put together a radio ad that led with *Mother Jones*'s money and politics coverage: Did you, listener, know that Republican speaker Newt Gingrich and Democratic minority leader Richard Gephardt had each taken two hundred thousand dollars from an identical list of corporate political action committees? OK, so it's not the Budweiser lizards. We were ready to go with the ad.

Hold on. The ABC standards and practices division said it wouldn't allow the ad on the air. The ad is defamatory, ABC said. What's defamatory? we asked. It's all true. The information was from the Federal Election Commission, public records. Who's defamed?

It's too controversial, ABC countered. You can't run the ad.

It damned sure ought to be controversial to have

the leaders of both parties on the take from an identical pack of hyenas. But too controversial? Where was standards and practices when ABC's *20/20* gave Jeffrey Dahmer's prom date a turn on national TV? Controversy per se was hardly the problem. More likely, ABC wanted to avoid rocking the boat of the men who were ushering the telecommunications act through Congress.

It gets worse. In March 1996, a few months after my encounter with ABC's standards and practices, Congress was considering whether to charge broadcasters a licensing fee for the rights to a new broadcast spectrum, rights that Common Cause estimated were worth about seventy billion dollars. During this debate, a prime-time TV commercial appeared in millions of homes. The ad showed a trio of TV sets playing *Seinfeld, David Letterman,* and *Jeopardy.* One by one, as a voiceover warns that the government is about to impose a "TV tax," the sets go dark, implying that the tax would end free TV as we know it. There was, of course, no TV tax. But the spot's toll-free number generated thousands of calls, a nice demonstration of how the broadcast industry can use paid ads to manipulate public opinion, all the while effectively banning unions, Indians, *Mother Jones,* and other troublemakers from the airwaves.

Of course, the messages from the troublemakers are unsettling, threatening to the homogenous view of the world we derive from our news and entertainment media. That's the point. The future we're being shown isn't totalitarian and cold. It's seductive, bright, full of entertainment and diversions. Far be it from any programming, even the news, to present a view of the world fundamentally at odds with that consumer paradise.

In the preface of his book *Amusing Ourselves to Death,* Neil Postman compared the bleak totalitarian future of George Orwell's *1984* to the future predicted in Aldous Huxley's *Brave New World.* Postman wrote:

"What Orwell feared were those who would ban books. What Huxley feared was that there would be no reason to ban a book, for there would be no one who wanted to read one. Orwell feared those who would deprive us of information. Huxley feared those who would give us so much that we would be reduced to passivity and egoism. Orwell feared that the truth would be concealed from us. Huxley feared the truth would be drowned out in a sea of irrelevance."

Let's look at what I've posited so far. Our media companies have been diverted from substantive, public-interest reporting by the chase for bigger audiences and profit. Reporters and editors find it easier and more rewarding to conform to a master narrative than to take risks. A cartel of giant, profit-driven companies is on course to swallow whatever remains of public discourse. And many of the rest of us are happily tuning in to the national soap opera and amusing ourselves to death.

You know, my wife gives me a hard time about this. She says the tag line for our magazine should be: *Mother Jones: Things Are Even Worse Than You Thought.* Sometimes a close look at deeper truths makes even me want to go home, pop a brewski, plop on the couch, and watch *Seinfeld* reruns. Come to think of it, I could watch the news. I wonder what's happening with Marv Albert anyway? I think the Guinness World Records show is rerunning its piece on the world's biggest tumors. Maybe I can catch that.

But I can't do that. And I doubt you can either.

I was honored recently to attend the ceremony for the Goldman Environmental Awards. The Goldman awards are presented annually to brave environmental activists on six continents, and the ceremony is always deeply moving. This year I was struck by what seemed like a common theme in the comments of these heroes and heroines. After the prize recipients stepped forward and recounted the battles they were fighting and the staggering obstacles and injustices in their way, several concluded their remarks by saying, in effect, if I can just get this story told, if I can just get my story *into the media,* other people will recognize the injustice and come to our side. You have to wonder, is the media listening? Will the rest of us ever hear those stories? Will we have the facts, from all sides, to come to our own judgments about these activists and their concerns?

The backbone of our democracy is a free and informed public. But what is informed? Most of us are bombarded with information. More than any previous generation on earth, we have a vast selection of channels at hand and more "news" than any one of us could possibly absorb. Still, something critical is missing. Without a press that puts the information in context, that helps us see shades of gray, that shows us where power lies, what it's doing, and how we can respond, without that, we are uninformed—and the democratic premise starts to fall apart.

My intent isn't to feed your cynicism. It's to get you agitated enough to start changing things. Here's my three-step advice. First, think critically about what's presented as news. Switch on your crap detector. Remember, quantity isn't the problem. (Taking it to the extreme, Danny Schecter, veteran news dissector, says, "The more you watch, the less you know.") Pay attention to where the holes in the news are, to where the dots don't connect, to the perspectives that haven't been heard from, to the obvious questions that haven't even been asked, much less answered.

Second, diversify your media diets. Mary Harris "Mother" Jones herself said, "Read, and educate yourself for the coming conflicts." As bleak as the commercial news situation is, it's still possible to keep informed. There are some great alternatives to the brain candy. Read, or listen to, *Mother Jones, The Nation,* Jim Hightower's *Low Down, Extra!, Adbusters,* Pacifica Radio's *Democracy Now, Rachel's Environment and Health Weekly,* Free Speech TV, community radio, and dozens of cool listserves and websites. You'll not only be doing yourself a favor, but if you actually subscribe to one or a few of these news sources, you'll help keep the alternative presses and cameras rolling. Staying free from advertiser pressure means that these news providers depend on readers and listeners paying their way.

Third: As a Bay Area radio guru, Scoop Nisker, says, "If you don't like the news, go out and make some of your own." I mean that two ways. After you broaden your media diet, start to act on what you learn. Vote, write, make trouble, make change, get together with like-minded others and let the Big Boys and Girls hear you. The nouveau robber barons are emboldened by nothing so much as ignorance and apathy. The good news, such as it is, is that the ripoffs these days are so massive and so appalling that even a modest public outcry is often sufficient to slow them down.

There's another way to make news, too. Become a producer of news. At *Mother Jones* we work hard to make sure that we're telling our stories in a way that makes real people want to read them. There's no point to being brilliantly informed journalists in the virtuous wilderness. The news isn't a trivia contest; it's the medium of democracy. We need to connect the information we have with people who can use it. To people who have kids and jobs, maybe two or three jobs, and damned little time. To folks who are suspicious of what they're getting from the commercial media but who may be suspicious of the alternatives, too. So, if you're among those who aspire to be journalists and publishers, I want to issue a double challenge: Keep your standards high and tell your stories as if you care that someone reads them.

8.
Follow the Bouncing Ball

How the Caged Bird Learns to Sing

By John Leonard

Victor Navasky, publisher of The Nation, *called his friend John Leonard, the distinguished essayist and critic, "the least self-censored person in the country." Even so, as Leonard recounted his career writing "for almost anyone who ever asked me," he also outlined a very personal series of pressures that he has confronted from time to time, some external—pressures from editors, producers, and friends—and some internal, as he balanced the advantages of staying with one employer with the presumed advantages of going to another. A color television set entered into one such debate.*

Leonard is media critic for CBS Sunday Morning, *the television critic for* New York *magazine, and book critic for* The Nation. *His books include* The Naked Martini; This Pen for Hire; The Last Innocent White Man in America; Smoke & Mirrors: Violence, Television and Other American Cultures; *and, in 1999,* When the Kissing Had to Stop: Cult Studs, Khmer Newts, Langley Spooks, Techno Geeks, Video Drones, Author Gods, Serial Killers, Vampire Media, Alien Sperm Suckers, Satanic Therapists, and Those of Us Who

Hold a Left-Wing Grudge in the Post-Toasties New World Hip-Hop.

Like a tribal warrior in the Ramayana, throwing dice, juiced on soma, I want to tell some stories and brood out loud. But it's tricky. My favorite stories are all about what *they* did to me. What I've done to myself, I am inclined to repress, sublimate, or rationalize. Once upon a time, I was a Wunderkind. Now I'm an Old Fart. In between I've done time at the *National Review,* Pacifica Radio and *The Nation;* the *New York Times* and Condé Nast; *New York* magazine during and after Rupert Murdoch; NPR and CBS. I was a columnist for *Esquire,* whenever Dwight Macdonald failed to turn in his politics essay; at the old weekly *Life* before it died for *People*'s sins; at *Newsweek* before the *Times* made me stop; at *Ms.* during its Australian aboriginal incarnation; and at *New York Newsday* before it was so rudely "disappeared" by a Times Mirror CEO fresh to journalism from the Hobbesian underworlds of microwave popcorn and breakfast cereal sugar-bombs. And I've written for almost anyone who ever asked me at newspapers like the *Washington Post, Los Angeles Times,* and the *Boston Globe* and at magazines like *Harper's* and *The Atlantic, Vogue* and *Playboy.* I like to think of myself as having published in the *New York Review of Books,* the *New Statesman, Yale Review,* and *Tikkun.* But there was also *TV Guide.*

This sounds less careerist than sluttish. It is, however, a sluttishness probably to be expected of someone who had to make a living after he discovered that the novels he *reviewed* were a lot better than the novels he *wrote.* We may belong to what the poet Paul Valéry called "the delirious professions," by which Valéry meant "all those trades whose main tool is one's opinion of one's self, and whose raw material is the opinion others have of you." But reporters, critics, and cultural journalists, no less than publicists, are caged birds in a corporate canary cage. Looking back, I see that what I required of my employers was that they cherish my every word, *and leave me alone!* If I understand what Warren Beatty was trying to tell us in the movie *Reds,* it is that John Reed only soured on the Russian Revolution after they fucked with his copy.

On the other hand, as Walter Benjamin once explained:

"The great majority of intellectuals—particularly in the arts—are in a desperate plight. The fault lies, however, not with their character, pride, or inaccessibility. Journalists, novelists, and literati are for the most part ready for every compromise. It's just that they do not realize it. And this is the reason for their failures. Because they do not know, or want to know, that they are venal, they do not understand that they should separate out those aspects of their opinions, experiences, and modes of behavior that might be of interest to the market. Instead, they make it a point of honor to be wholly themselves on every issue. Because they want to be sold, so to speak, only 'in one piece,' they are as unsalable as a calf that the butcher will sell to the housewife only as an undivided whole."

I throw in Walter Benjamin, the German-Jewish philosopher and critic, who killed himself a step ahead of Hitler, to startle academics. Having been to too many conferences where working reporters and media theorists reach an angry adjournment of minds before the first coffee break, I seek to ingratiate myself. If it'll help to wear a Heidegger safari jacket, Foucault platform heels, Lacan epaulets, and a Walter Benjamin boutonniere, I'm willing to bring the Frankfurters and the French fries. Indeed, the production process of every major newsgathering organization can be thought of—in Foucault's terms—as an allegory of endless domination, like hangmen torturing murderers, or doctors locking up deviants. Whether they know it consciously or not, these organizations are in the "corrective technologies" business of beating down individuals to "neutralize" their "dangerous states," to create "docile bodies and obedient souls." How we escape their "numbing codes of discipline," if we ever do, is more problematic. Somehow, art, dreams, drugs, madness, "erotic transgression," "secret self-ravishment" and "going postal" seldom add up to an "insurrection of unsubjugated knowledges." I like to think of myself as Patsy Cline. I sang the same old country songs before I ever got to the Grand Ole Opry. After the Grand Ole Opry, I can always go back to the honkytonks.

Another paradigm is sociobiological. Everything is hardwired, from the behavior of ants, beetles, Egyptian fruit bats, and adhesive-padded geckos to the role of women, the caste system in India, the IQ test scores of black schoolchildren, and the hierarchy of the newsroom. If the people on top of this Chain of Being are mostly male and mostly pale, in the missionary position, talk to Darwin about it. They've been Naturally Selected. Moreover, inside such a white-noise system, there is a positive-feedback loop between nature and nurture, thousands of teensy units of obedience training called "culturgens," dictating what societies can and can't do, obsessing in favor of patriarchy and objectivity, deploring socialism and bad taste. Having ceded ultimate authority, on the one hand, to the credentialed nitwits of the mini-sciences and on the other to the chirpy gauchos of the media pampas, we may thus find it difficult, ever again, to think through dilemmas of personal conscience, which look a lot like bad career moves.

Molly Ivins, who was fired from the *New York Times* after saying "chickenplucker" in its pages, has admitted that if she ever dies, what it will say on her tombstone is "She Finally Made a Shrewd Career Move." Molly also claims that she's actually played on the jukebox a country-and-western song called, "I'm Going Back to Dallas to See If There Could Be Anything Worse Than Losing You."

A third paradigm is novelistic. It's amazing to me how much the controlled environments of both CBS and the *New York Times* resemble Tsau, the utopian community on a Botswana sand dune in Norman Rush's *Mating,* with windmills, boomslangs, dung carts, abacus lessons, militant nostalgia, ceramic death masks, "Anti-Imperialist Lamentations," a Mother Committee, and an ostrich farm. And how similar the plantations of Murdoch and Newhouse are to Orwell's *Animal Farm* and Kafka's *Penal Colony.* Whereas Pacifica Radio and *The Nation* bring to mind Voltaire's *Candide.* On these margins, where everyone is paid so poorly that office politics are ideologized into matters of first principle, a little more self-censorship might actually be a good idea. I am reminded of what Amos Oz said about the Israeli Left in *The Slopes of Lebanon:*

"The term Phalaganist is derived from the Greek word 'phalanx.' The phalanx, in the Greek and Roman armies, was a unique battle formation. The soldiers were arranged in a closed-square formation, their backs to one another and their faces turned toward an enemy who could neither outflank nor surprise them, because in this formation the men gave full cover to one another in every direction. The lances and spears pointed outward, of course, in all four directions.

"The moderate, dovish Israel left sometimes resembles a reverse phalanx: a square of brave fighters, their backs to the whole world and their faces and their sharpened, unsheathed pens turned on one another."

So much for the Big Pixel. As I intuit the ulterior purpose of this series, what you really want are the prurient details. And, stuck as I am on my periphery of books, movies, and television programs, I can't tell you for sure whether Tom Friedman, when he covered the State Department for the *Times,* should have played tennis with the secretary of state. Or if Brit Hume, when he covered the White House for ABC, should have played tennis with President Bush. Or if Rita Beamish of the Associated Press should have jogged with George. Or if it was appropriate for George and Barbara to stop by and be videotaped at a media dinner party in the home of Albert Hunt, the Washington bureau chief of the *Wall Street Journal,* and his wife, Judy Woodruff, then of the *MacNeil/Lehrer NewsHour* and now on CNN. Or if one reason Andrea Mitchell, who covered Congress for NBC, showed up so often in the presidential box at the Kennedy Center was that she just happened to be living with Alan Greenspan, the chairman of the Federal Reserve Board. Nor can I be absolutely positive that there's something deeply compromised about George Will's still ghostwriting speeches for Jesse Helms during his trial period as a columnist for the *Washington Post* and prepping Ronald Reagan for one of his debates with Jimmy Carter, then reviewing Reagan's performance in his column, and later on writing a speech Reagan delivered to the House of Commons. Or about Morton Kondracke's and Robert Novak's collecting thousands of dollars from the Republican Party for advice to a gathering of governors. Or John McLaughlin's settling one sexual harassment suit out of court, facing the prospect of at least two more—and nevertheless permitting himself to savage Anita Hill on his own *McLaughlin Group*. Or Henry Kissinger, on ABC television and in his syndicated newspaper column, defending Deng Xiao-ping's behavior during the Tiananmen Square massacre, without telling us that he, Henry, and his private consultancy firm had a substantial financial stake in the Chinese status quo.

For that matter, who knows deep down in our heart of hearts whether the nuclear power industry will ever get the critical coverage it deserves from NBC, which happens to be owned by General Electric, which happens to manufacture nuclear-reactor turbines; or from CBS, which is owned by Westinghouse, which happens to manufacture not only reactors for submarines and aircraft carriers but also nuclear power plants themselves? Or if *TV Guide,* owned by Rupert Murdoch, will ever savage a series on the Fox network, also owned by Rupert Murdoch, who is meanwhile busy canceling any HarperCollins books that might annoy the Chinese with whom he is dickering for a satellite television deal? Or whether

ABC, owned by Disney, will ever report anything embarrassing about Michael Eisner, the Mikado of Mousedom? It wasn't the fault of the journalists at ABC's *20/20* that Cap Cities settled the Philip Morris suit before selling out to Disney. Nor was it the fault of journalists at *60 Minutes* that CBS killed another antismoking segment; it was the fault instead of the legal department, on behalf of Larry Tisch, on the eve of his profitable sale of the network to Westinghouse. But nobody quit either, did they, not even aggrieved producer Lowell Bergman until two years later. Any more than any of the Inside-the-Beltway blisterpack-bubbles on the all-Monica-all-the-time cable yakshows quit in humiliation, and renounced their lecture fees, after they were totally wrong in public about everything from the 1998 congressional elections all the way back to the 1989 collapse of the nonprofit police states of Eastern Europe.

Stop me before I go on about the petroleum industry and public television's shamefully inadequate coverage of the Exxon Valdez oil spill, not to mention Shell Oil's ravening of Nigeria. How suspicious is it that so many Random House books were excerpted in the *New Yorker* back when Harry Evans ran the publishing house, his wife, Tina Brown, ran the magazine, and all of them were wholly owned subsidiaries of Si Newhouse. Is anybody keeping tabs on what *Time, People,* and *Entertainment Weekly* have to say about Warner Brothers movies? What else should we expect in a brand-named, theme-parked country where the whole visual culture is a stick in the eye, one big sell of booze, gizmos, insouciance, lifestyles, and combustible emotions? Where the big-screen re-release of George Lucas's *Star Wars* trilogy is brought to you by Doritos and the associated sale of stuffed Yodas, Muppet minotaurs, trading cards, video games, and a six-foot-tall fiberglass Storm Trooper for five thousand dollars? Where the newest James Bond is less a movie than a music-video marketing campaign for luxury cars, imported beers, mobile phones, and gold credit cards? Where Coke and Pepsi duke it out in grammar schools, and Burger King shows up on the sides of the yellow buses that cart our kids to those schools, in whose classrooms they'll be handed curriculum kits sprinkled with the names of sneaker companies and breakfast cereals? Where there is a logo, a patent, a trademark, or a copyright on everything from our pro athletes to our childhood fairy tales, and Oprah is sued for twelve million dollars by a Texas beef lobby for "disparaging" blood on a bun during a talk-show segment on spongiform encephalopathy and Creutzfeldt-Jakob disease?

And where, I might add, all of us "delirious professionals" sign away, in perpetuity, our intellectual property rights, our firstborn children, and our double helix to synergizing media monopolies that will probably downsize our asses before the pension plan kicks in. Karl Marx has made a mini-comeback on the hundredth birthday of his *Communist Manifesto.*

But years before he wrote the manifesto he was overheard to say: "Since money, as the existing and active concept of value, confounds and exchanges everything, it is the universal *confusion and transposition* of all things, the inverted world, the confusion and transposition of all natural and human qualities." In other words, if money's the only way we keep score, every other human relation is corrupted.

Let me now get up-close and personal. Not long after I took charge of the *New York Times Book Review,* in the early 1970s, I had a surprise visitor. Lester Markel, the editor who had invented the Sunday *Times* with all its many sections, the eighth-floor Charlemagne who was rumored like Idi Amin to have stocked his fridge with the severed heads of his many enemies, liked to stop in and sit a while, like a bound galley or an urgent memo. This was because, after his forced retirement, he wasn't welcome in anyone else's office. Alone among the editors of the various Sunday sections, I had never worked for or been wounded by him. I was, besides, a fresh ear. It was rather like chewing the early-morning fat with El Cid himself, propped up on a horse but secretly dead.

It turned out that Markel was writing his memoirs. And he was having trouble finding a publisher. I made some suggestions and some calls. Never mind the propriety of the editor of the *Times Book Review* lobbying a publisher on behalf of an author with a manuscript for sale. We achieved a contract. And I didn't see Markel for months. Until, of course, galleys of his book came in. So did he, with suggestions for reviewers. That's when I had to acquaint him with the notion and the etiquette of disinterested criticism. After which, he fixed me with the blood-freezing eye of a basilisk. And I still had the problem of finding a reviewer who would pay Markel his due as a giant of yore, while not at the same time neglecting to mention his memoir's tendency toward stupefying portentousness—a reviewer who would not only be fair, but who would be perceived as fair by everybody else. I'd already been burned by my predecessor, who left for me for my very first issue a review of the memoirs of another retired *Times* executive, Turner Catledge, by one of his best friends at the University of Mississippi.

Let me digress for a moment to observe that a *Times* executive who wrote a book could always count on generous review attention so long as he was retired. As Wilfrid Sheed reminded us in *Max Jamison,* his novel about criticism: "They were soft, affable people who wouldn't hurt you because they couldn't bear to be hurt themselves. Paternal organizations were built on great piles of spiritual blubber." But the same generosity has not until recently been true lower down the totem pole, for the serfs. These serfs write a lot of books. When Christopher Lehmann-Haupt and I alternated as daily critics, we looked at these books the same as we'd look at any other. If we liked it or it seemed at least symptomatic of something compelling in the larger culture that we wanted to sermonize about, we'd review it. If not, we didn't. Pretty simple. You may have noticed that in recent years, books by *Times* employees are farmed out to freelancers. They are never reviewed by in-house critics. This, we are told, is to avoid the appearance of conflict of interest. Sounds good. Never mind just how often these outside reviews are actually negative. (I recall two in ten years.) But have you also noticed that this new policy means that all books by *Times* writers are always reviewed in the daily paper? Minus Saturdays and Sundays, there are 261 book reviews published in the daily *New York Times* every year. There are sixty-five thousand new books published in the United States every year. Some of these books are more equal than others in the paper of record.

Back to Lester Markel, and the paragon I needed to review him. That paragon, clearly, was Ben Bagdikian, a hugely respected, eminently fair-minded, award-winning reporter who had gone to academe. Also a gent. He agreed to do the review. Then, when the days before publication of Markel's memoir dwindled down to a precious few, Bagdikian called, in a pickle. He had been hired by the *Washington Post.* And the *Washington Post* had a policy that prohibited any of its employees from writing for the *New York Times.* (The *New York Times,* in fact, had the same policy in reverse, which is why it told me to stop writing a TV column for *Newsweek,* which was owned by the *Washington Post.*) Anyway, Ben was stuck. Well, I needed to know, was he still willing to do the review if I could get the *Post* to make an exception in this one instance, in which of course we had entered into an agreement before he sold his soul to the company store? Yes, he said; he'd already done the work.

So I called Bill McPherson, editor of the *Washington Post Book World,* whom I knew from literary cocktail parties, explaining my Markel problem and beseeching him to intercede on my behalf with *Post* poobah Ben Bradlee, whom I had met once at a Harvard Crimson alumni softball game and another time, I'm sorry to say, in the Hamptons. A long week passed. Finally McPherson called. Bradlee would relent about Bagdikian, on one condition. What was that condition? It was that I, personally, agree to review a book of Bradlee's choice for the *Washington Post.* Done, I said, figuring I'd square it somehow with the *Times.* Which book? Bradlee hadn't made up his mind. So I got my Bagdikian review, which was as scrupulous as I'd hoped, and published it, which stung Markel to furious rebuttal in a letter to the editor, which received from Bagdikian a mildly puzzled response, which correspondence dragged on intolerably until I called it off, after which I never saw Lester Markel in my office again.

But that's not the point of this story. A year later the phone rang, and it was McPherson, and he said: "Bradlee's calling in his chit." Which book, I asked?

Well—and McPherson was embarrassed—Sally Quinn was about to publish a book on her year at CBS. That was the one. Many of you are too young to remember that there was a Ben Bradlee before Jason Robards played him in the film version of *All the President's Men,* and that this Ben Bradlee left his wife for Sally Quinn, a reporter for the *Washington Post* Style section, and that this Sally Quinn then left the *Post,* very briefly, for a CBS morning show about which most TV critics had been savage, although at least one of us, me, had been sort of kind in *Life* magazine.

Nor is the point of this story that I refused to write that book review. The point is that Lester Markel had no business in my office, that I had no business trying to find him a publisher or to arrange for a judicious review—and that Bradlee's way is how the big boys play the game: while making sure your girlfriend gets a talked-about review, at the same time stick it to your principal competitor. Only Bagdikian emerges with honor. Some years later I said that to a class in the ethics of journalism that Bagdikian taught at Berkeley. The students in the class, including my own son, were amused at an anecdote starring their professor, but didn't get the ethics of it. It seemed sort of locker-room to them, as it seemed to grad students from the Columbia journalism school in a seminar I taught myself. They were all children of the triumph of a glossier idea of journalism that postures in front of experience, rather than engaging it; that looks in its cynical opportunism for an angle, or a spin, or a take, instead of consulting compass-points of principle; that strikes attitudes like matches, the better to admire their wiseguy profile in the mirror of the slicks.

I am aware that my own regard for books is overly worshipful—one part Hegel, one part Tinkerbell, Sacred Text, Pure Thought, and Counter-Geography—at a time when most of the dead trees in the chain stores have titles like "How I Lost Weight, Found God, Smart-Bombed Ragheads, and Changed My Sexual Preference in the Bermuda Triangle." But I also know it's as hard to write a good book as a bad one, and a lot easier to review one than achieve one, and if book critics in mainstream newspapers and magazines seem to have appointed themselves the hall monitors of an unruly schoolboy culture—this one gets a pass to go to the lavatory; that one must sit in the corner wearing a dunce cap—then it's a condescension and contempt passed down and internalized from bosses like Bradlee for whom the whole thing is a whimsical scam.

I've yet to meet a media boss who didn't think all of the books of all of his friends deserved a sympathetic review. Nor have I met a media boss who thought I should ever use as a reviewer anybody who has ever criticized him or his friends. Max Frankel, who accused me in his autobiography of trying to turn the *Times Book Review* into a combination of the *Village Voice* and the *New York Review of Books,* once called me on the carpet for using Timothy Crouse as a reviewer because Crouse had made fun of his Washington press corps friends in *The Boys on the Bus.* Abe Rosenthal not only called me on the carpet for saying nice things on the daily book page about I. F. Stone and Nat Hentoff, but suspended me from the job after I panned a book, *The Second Stage,* by his friend Betty Friedan. The next thing I knew, the *Times* had killed a sports column I wrote, during the pro football strike, in which I pointed out that the head of the players union, Ed Garvey, used to spook for the CIA. This of course goes beyond the butthole politics of the buddy-bond. It's over in another office, where foreign editor Jimmy Greenfield killed a "Private Lives" column I wrote about the Philippines, back when the Frog Prince Ferdinand and his Dragon Lady were still in charge, and playwrights like Ben Cervantes were still in prison, and Greenfield in New York knew more about it than I did in Manila, where a goon in a blue jumpsuit followed me out of the Palace of Culture, all over the landfill in the Bay, into a lurid jeepney.

This sounds like whining. It *is* whining. A primary characteristic of any news organization is the subculture of the crybaby gripe. (As if we ever had it harder than a schoolteacher or a factory worker or a farmer or a cop; as if we had ever been threatened with redundancy, much less a firing squad; as if our slippery slide weren't down into a wad of cotton candy.) And so I could go on about what happened to Richard Eder as the drama critic, and to Ray Bonner at El

Mozote, and to the class-action suit by the women of the *Times,* for which I was deposed, and to Roger Wilkins, who quit the paper to write his own book (which I probably shouldn't have reviewed), and to Jerzy Kosinksi, and Neil Sheehan, and Attica, and AIDS. I could even tell you about having to write my review of the first volume of Henry Kissinger's memoirs two days early, so that it could go all the way to the top to be vetted, after which I was permitted to suggest that some of us, on hearing from Henry that his only sleepless night in public service had been on the eve of his first mixer with the Red Chinese debutantes, thought maybe he should have tossed and turned more often. I might mention a review of Judith Exner's memoir about being passed around from Frank Sinatra to Sam Giancana to John F. Kennedy, which had to be published in the *SoHo News* instead of the *Times.* And I still don't know who cut the last two paragraphs of a review I wrote about a couple of JFK assassination books in 1970; those two paragraphs, asking questions about the sloppiness of the Warren Commission Report, simply vanished between the first edition and the last, an incriminating fact on microfilm that is periodically rediscovered by paranoids who write me letters that I dutifully forward to Abe.

No wonder that when Ed Diamond was researching his book on the *Times* and mentioned my name to John Rothman, the keeper of the archives, Rothman sniffed: "Some people just aren't good *Times*-

men." He promptly edited himself: "Some people aren't good *organizational* men." I could live happily with that had I quit in 1970. But I allowed myself to be promoted instead, and stayed another twelve years. When I finally left, it wasn't over an issue of principle. Those of us who go over the wall—who leave the Catholic Church or the Communist Party or the *New York Times*—usually decide at last to jump because of something small. You have swallowed a whole history of whoppers, but there is a fatigue about your faith. Without any warning, the elastic snaps, and you are hurled out of the closed system into empty space, and your renunciation, arrived at by so many increments, looks almost capricious.

In my case, I decided to believe that the brand-new *Vanity Fair* would be a serious magazine, as did many of my friends. And so we entered the halls of Condé Nast like the children who followed Stephen of Vendome south to Marseilles in 1212, expecting the Mediterranean to part like the Red Sea, allowing us to pass over to the Promised Land. We were sold instead into slavery in Egypt. Actually, I was in Jerusalem writing a story on Peace Now when people from the magazine called the King David hotel to tell me to come back, that they had fired the editor who hired me and it wasn't going to be a Peace Now kind of magazine anymore. When we leap over the wall, we always imagine that *they,* whoever *they* are, will love us more in the outside world. They will love us just as much, or as little, as we serve their interest.

To finish with the *Times:* When I told them I was quitting, first they said that I had promised I never would. Never say never. Then they explained, "The *Times* is a centrist institution, and you are not a centrist." Fair enough, although the center sure had moved since they hired me directly out of the antiwar movement. Finally, they screamed at me: "We made you! You'd be nothing without the *Times!*" This surprised. It had never before occurred to me that they'd published what I wrote, two or three times a week, out of the kindness of their hearts, that we hadn't somehow been *even* every day. For years after, I thought about this departing as Freudian-dysfunctional. Maybe they wanted to be our fathers. Maybe we wanted them to be our fathers. Oedipus! Peter Pan! Then I began to wonder whether there wasn't about our servitude elements of an abusive marriage—tantrums, fists, and fear; excuses and apologies and denials; dependency and self-loathing—battered wives and battered writers. Now, contemplating all the ghosts in this denial machine, I'm inclined to remember the theater tickets and the stock options and all the cocktail parties I got invited to as if I were important.

Paul Krassner, the Yippie editor of *The Realist,* once explained to a conference on the media and the environment how to tell the difference between "news" and "dreaming." When you see something you don't believe, you should flap your arms like wings. If you seem then to be flying, it's a dream. I've been going on for a very long time and haven't even got to CBS, where I've spent the last eleven years. Before I was hired at *Sunday Morning,* I asked for a free hand in choosing which television programs I reviewed, regardless of network. My own credibility was at stake. I was assured of a hands-off policy. That was three presidents of CBS News ago.

In fact, for the first seven or so years, I was, if not ignored, then rather negligently embraced as a sort of punctuation mark, a change of rhythm, or a passionate parenthesis, in one of the vanishingly few network news programs to embody and cherish old-fashioned journalistic standards. When *Sunday Morning* wasn't thinking about culture, its splendid idea of news was to notice that, hey, here's a social problem; here are some people trying to do something about it; why don't we spend eight whole minutes seeing if what they're doing actually works? Those who only recall Charles Kuralt as a kind of Johnny Appleseed of avuncular anecdotes and homespun decencies need reminding that he'd been a fine reporter in Southeast Asia and Latin America; that he went to China at the time of Tiananmen, where his take was very different from Dr. Kissinger's; that he expressed his doubts, over the air, about the Gulf War. It's not just that Kuralt listened better than most people talk; he was an exacerbated conscience of his profession. He even refused to appear on the *Murphy Brown* sitcom: "I don't know where the line is," he told me, "but that's crossing it." With his passing, we are diminished in heart and jumping beans.

But the world of television journalism has been changing, not since O. J. or Monica or the Internet, but ever since it was discovered that news can be a profit center. I should have got an inkling my first year on-air, when I reviewed a public-TV documentary on Edward R. Murrow, whose valor and grace made him our very own tragic hero. Emerging on CBS television from the radio and the war, he grasped the new medium's power to modify the way a nation thought about itself, then watched helplessly as that medium pawned that power to the ad agencies, and smoked himself to death. He even *looked* like Albert Camus, the Shadow Man of the French Resistance—Bogart with a microphone. We were reminded in the documentary that he'd been stunned when the gates of Buchenwald were opened. That he cared so much about words, he often forgot to look at the camera. That he made up *See It Now* as he went along, forever over-budget. That after his famous demolition job on Joe McCarthy, Alcoa dropped its sponsorship of *See It Now* and William Paley, the Big Eye in the Black Rock Sky, turned against his best-known reporter, bumping the program from the prime-time schedule. That in his last few years at CBS before he resigned in 1961 there were many more *Person to Person* chats with the likes of Marilyn Monroe than there had ever been exposes like "Harvest of Shame," on the plight of migrant farmworkers. What I should have noticed at the time was the allegorical nature of the Murrow story. In every institution of our society, but especially the media, there have always been brilliant young men—and men almost all of them have always been—who find surrogate fathers as Murrow found Paley. For a while in this relationship of privilege, patronage, and protections, these young men imagine that they can go on being brilliant, on their own terms, forever, immune to the bottom-line logic of a corporate culture which, for its own reasons, has surrounded and preserved them in aspic. We are not at all fathers and sons; we are landlords and tenants; owners and pets. It shouldn't surprise the brilliant young men, and yet it always surprises the brilliant young men, when the party is over and the pets are put to sleep.

I am once again peripheral to the larger story. When CBS lost pro football, and then a bunch of affiliate stations, to Rupert Murdoch's Fox, everybody freaked. One Thursday, I went in as usual to submit a script for TelePrompTing, record the voice-over for my tape package, and go home again to watch more television. Later that afternoon, the executive producer called. The president of CBS News then—he is gone now, or how likely is it that I'd be telling you this?—had seen that I was reviewing a TV movie forthcoming on Fox, a feature-length reprise of the old *Alien Nation* sci-fi series, and he'd hit the roof. He had to go to an affiliates' meeting the next Monday morning. They would chew his ears off after hearing their own network promote a program on the evil empire's competing schedule. I said that I had been specifically promised that this would never happen; that anyway, and never mind my poor powers to cloud anybody's mind, including A. C. Nielsen's, it couldn't really be my problem if the corporation's stock went up or down, or if the president of news had to go to an affiliates' meeting or a therapist. I was told they'd get back to me, and late that night they did. The president was adamant. I guess I'll have to quit, I said. Don't be silly and overreactive, I was told. Then the executive producer *handled* me. A month before I had proposed a piece about Doris Lessing, on the occasion of her seventy-fifth birthday and the publication of the first volume of her autobiography. Nobody had been interested. Now, if I wanted to sit down immediately and write it up, they'd run it on Sunday in place of *Alien Nation.* Quid pro quo, Q.E.D., ad nauseam, and beat vigorously.

It occurs to me now that thirty years ago *Life* magazine rejected a "Cyclops" column of mine describing Richard Nixon as a jack-in-the-box television president: Surprise! Look what Daddy brought home from the Cold War! A secret bombing of Cambodia! Then, too, I vented at length to a sympathetic but helpless editor. The next day, *Life* magazine sent me a brand-new color television set, my very first. All night long, with my children, I shopped for friendship in the gorgeous beer commercials. So Doris Lessing is a sort of color television set.

If I couldn't review the network competition, I refused to review CBS, although cable and public television were still fair game. So what followed Doris Lessing was some strong encouragement for me to branch out more, into movies and books. This made rationalizing easy. More books is always better. Free movies spice it up, even while you quickly realize that TV is more various and interesting. CBS still, amazingly, lets me say exactly what I want to about abortion and capital punishment, racism and homophobia, misogyny and war. (We are hired for our stylistic bag of tricks, our jetstream vapor trails, not our politics. Had my politics been right-wing instead of left, somebody else would have overpaid for this vapor.) And there's a new president of CBS News. If I combine network shows in a thematic clump, one from column A, two from column B, I'm back in the consumer-guide business. What's more, this wandering in the wilderness has led me to realize that we end up, in the cultural-journalism business, reviewing the buzz more often than the artifact itself. That the more money spent on promotion, the more attention we have to pay, no matter what our opinion. If it is heavily hyped, it automatically becomes newsworthy. Never mind the little movie with the distracting subtitles; nobody else will review it, either. So I'm smarter now. Flap your arms if you think you're dreaming.

The sad thing is that, since now at last I am old enough to be *too* old, almost, for network television—a demographic undesirable to the ad agencies—my very senior citizenship means that my children are out of college, I own the roof over my head, and I ought to be immune to the terrors of authenticity. I need not be beholden to those who choose to leak on me, nor belong to any hard-wired paradigm that imagines itself a fourth branch of the government, even a separate country, with its own pomp, protocols, dress codes, foreign policy, and official secrets, lacking only its own anthem and maybe a helicopter beanie. And yet the *Times* paid for that house, CBS bought me a new kitchen, and in the last ten years I've vacationed in China, Egypt, Zimbabwe, and Tuscany. I've actually stayed in hotels like the Danieli in Venice, the Peninsula in Hong Kong, and the Oriental in Bangkok, in spite of the fact that I know I don't belong there—that you can take the boy out of his class, but not that class out of the boy.

This is the deepest censorship of the self, an upward mobility and a downward trajectory. Once upon a time way back in high school, we thought of reporters as private eyes. We thought of journalism as a craft instead of a club of professional perkies who worried about summer homes, Tuscan vacations, Jungian analysis, engraved invitations to Truman Capote parties, and private schools for our sensitive children. We scratched down an idea on a scrap of yellow paper, typed it up on an Underwood portable, took it below to the print shop, set it on a Linotype machine, read that type upside-down, ran off a proof on a flatbed press, and seemed somehow to connect brain and word, muscle and idea, hot lead and cool thought. But that was long before we got into the information-commodities racket, where we have more in common with Henry Kravis and Henry Kissinger than we do with papermakers and deliverymen, or those ABC technicians who were so alone, on strike, on Columbus Avenue. After which our real story is ourselves, at the Century Club or Elaine's or a masked ball charity scam—Oscar de la Renta, Alex Solzhenitsyn, and Leona Helmsley invite you to Feel Bad About the Boat People at the Museum of Modern Art—with plenty of downtime left over after we've crossed a picket line by phoning in our copy on the computer to make it to Yankee Stadium, where Boss Steinbrenner will lift us up by our epaulets to his skybox to consort with such presbyters of the Big Fix as Roy Cohn and Donald Trump, and you can't tell the pearls from the swine.